Life On The Farm:
Beyond The Garden

Judi Kotwas

Judi Kotwas

DEDICATION

For my husband Mike: My co-star in many stories, friend, my love, and my enduring inspiration.

For my daughter and best friend, Jessica: Whose accomplishments continue to far exceed my own, and who makes me proud every day.

For my parents, George and Olive Wise: Who raised me to face life with humor and a positive attitude, and to treat others with tolerance and gentleness.

 For my granddaughters, Juliana and Isabella: Who make me smile and allow me to view life all over again through fresh, young eyes.

For my son-in-law, Sean: Who treats my daughter like a precious treasure, and me as a friend.

And for my dear family, in-law family, and friends: Thanks for standing by me in this continuing pursuit of a dream.

Judi Kotwas

ACKNOWLEDGMENTS

My thanks to thinkexist.com for being a rich source of quotations from celebrities, authors, philosophers, and common folks with common sense.

My thanks to createspace.com for their guidance and assistance in bringing this book to realization.

My thanks to Brian Bailone, who shot some of the photographs featured in these stories, and who helped me to meet my musical idol, Adam Lambert – twice!.

My gratitude to Paula and Daryl Senft, owners of The Victorian Parlor tea room in Spring Grove, PA, for allowing me to feature their wonderful establishment in one of these stories, and for a truly excellent high tea. Learn more about them and their beautiful tea room at TheVictorianParlor.com.

Judi Kotwas

CONTENTS

Judi Kotwas

INTRODUCTION

My first book, "Life On The Farm: Out To Pasture," described how I arrived at retirement and navigated the process of transition to a new way of living. Now in book number two, I have my balance. Like riding a bike, it becomes easy with a little time and practice.

In his book, "The Shark and the Goldfish", author Jon Gordon said that if you think your best days are behind you, they are; and if you think your best days are ahead of you, they are. This is terrific news for me, because I still wake up each morning, thinking, "What's next?". Some days I catch myself thinking about my next career step, and what training I might require to achieve it. Well, Grandma Moses was older than I am when she began her career as a great artist. How's that for inspiration to keep climbing?

Sure, there are days when middle-aged aches and pains take a starring role, or when I look into the mirror with less than total joy, fully sympathetic to Nora Ephron's piece on aging, entitled "I Feel Bad About My Neck." Those are the days when I have to remind myself that sometimes the only way out of a bad place is through, and that sometimes the other side will be so glorious that I might be grateful for whatever got me there.

But most days, it is easy to recall that happiness really is an inside job, held apart from external circumstances or possessions. I rejoice again that, instead of making that long, daily commute to a desk in a cubicle with fabric walls, I get to watch the snow and ice fall down from inside my den window, wearing my pajamas and fuzzy slippers, with a hot mug of tea warming my hands cupped around it, and that there is time, at last, to paint the pictures held in my mind for so long, and to write stories such as the ones in this book.

I hope that, as you read, you will be entertained, lifted up and inspired. I hope that you find the time, now or sometime soon, to pursue your own dream.

Most of all, I wish you the happiness that comes from within.

1: A YEAR OF 356 DAYS?

"What the caterpillar calls the end of the world, the master calls a butterfly." - Richard Bach

This new year, 2012, is different from all of those preceding it. The coming of the year 2012 has unleashed a torrent of speculation about what lies ahead for the earth and mankind. And all because the Mayan calendar ends on December 21, 2012, 356 days into this year.

I remember the excitement and anxiety that many of us felt with the coming of the year 2000 not so long ago. Many 'experts' predicted chaos and the collapse of our electronic infrastructure because computers had not been programmed to roll the date from 19xx to 2xxx.

As a software engineer at a large corporation, I was working on solutions for some looming date-stamp problems with our older computers, and I knew that technical experts everywhere were working to prevent large-scale catastrophe with the turning of the calendar page.   Still, along with the anxiety there was an element of adventure, waiting to find out the full impact on the computer infrastructure that oversees scheduling, organization and data storage for the world in which we all now live.

Tempting fate, my husband and I made our first trip to Hawaii, joining his mother and siblings with their spouses and families to celebrate the turn of the new century in style. We had all decided that if we were going to get stranded somewhere when all the computer systems locked up, it might as well be in paradise. The clock ticked down the minutes on December 31, 1999, and fireworks filled the skies around the world as each time zone reached midnight. The ball dropped in Times Square as it always did. In Hawaii, we set off fireworks on the beach and toasted another year. At countless celebrations, the band played Auld Lang Syne and people shook hands, hugged and kissed. And in the computer world – nothing happened. No Armaggedon. Computer systems hummed steadily along, oblivious to the furor surrounding them. Software engineers around the world breathed a collective sigh of relief. Father Time had apparently loaded this particular pistol with blanks.

So here in 2012, we stand on the brink of another calendar-related fork in the road. Doomsday prophets predict that the world will end on December 21, 2012. More optimistic philosophers believe that December 21, 2012 will mark the dawning of the Age of Light, or Age of Consciousness, during which humans will evolve into a biologically conscious species capable

of holding and sharing the full light of unconditional
love. OK, a bit eccentric, but a view that I prefer to
the doomsday theory. The probable truth is that, just
as in 2000, nothing significant will occur and life will
continue in its usual pattern until the next fork in the
road.

For many of us, the beginning of each new year is a
threshold for a fresh start on our path to betterment.
I began writing this at 7:00 a.m. on New Year's Day,
2012, and as the sky grew lighter with the rising sun,
I reflected on this special New Year's Day.   Maybe
the world will end on December 21 as some pundits
have hypothesized.   I don't know if life will end for
me tomorrow; none of us knows. 2012 could last for
366 days (it is leap year), or 356, or maybe only 1
day. If I hear the clock ticking a little louder because
of the uniqueness of this year, it is a good thing,
because it reminds me that my time here is not
without limits, my days are precious and must be used
wisely.

So I've decided to make 2012 different from all the
years preceding it. I'm going to make extra efforts to
keep this year's resolutions. And because I want to
make a difference while I'm on this earth, I'm adding
a few extra checkpoints to the list. I want to be
kinder, more generous to those in need, more loving
to my family and friends, more forgiving to strangers
who inadvertently offend or annoy me, more devoted

to the actions and values that I believe in, and more centered on the spirituality that calls to the better self within me.

My wish for 2012 is for longevity, gratitude in happy times, strength in bad times, and grace in difficult times.   That is my wish for each of us.

Happy 2012!

2: EGGSHELLS AND EMPTY JARS

"Each generation, in turn, becomes the custodian rather than the absolute owner of our resources, and each generation has the obligation to pass this inheritance on to the future." – Charles Lindbergh

Whenever my mother-in-law comes to visit, shortly after she arrives at our house she always hands me a little tote bag. From her smile of anticipation and my pleased reaction, an outside observer would conclude that the bag contains a lovely gift. And so it does - a Ziploc baggie of clean eggshells and several empty glass jelly jars.

As the years pass, I become more aware of the fragile balance on our little planet. At mankind's beginning, the Creator charged us with stewardship of this world and all of its life forms, and I am a "custodian-of-our-environment" work in progress, increasingly mindful of how my actions affect the world around me. We each choose, consciously or subconsciously, the nature of our legacy to future generations, to either improve or diminish the earth in our time.

My husband Mike and I try to live in a way that will leave a beneficial legacy. We minimize our trash volume by re-using and recycling as much as possible, and we try to nurture our garden, especially my husband's prized tomato plants, in earth-friendly ways. Each year we learn a little more about the

7

various pests and diseases, and the best ways to fight back without harming the environment. In past years we lost a large portion of the tomato harvest to a number of causes, one of the worst being "blossom end rot." The primary cause is inadequate calcium in the soil, and there are a number of corrective additives sold by gardening centers, but most are filled with toxic chemicals.

Then we learned that clean eggshells can be ground into a powder and sprinkled around the tomato plants to add precious calcium to the soil and fight blossom end rot in a eco-friendly manner without residual harm. So now we save and freeze our empty eggshells all year - and I love to bake, so we use a lot of eggs. By spring, the baggies will be stacked high on the freezer shelves.

And in the spirit of re-use, we store emptied jelly jars in boxes in the basement until the next season of jam-making, to be cleaned, refilled, and transformed once again into little jars of love given to family and friends.

It would be less trouble to toss those empty jars and eggshells. The jars crowd the shelves in our basement storage room, and a year's worth of eggshells take up a lot of space in the freezer. But are we talkers, or do we walk the walk? So we save them.

My mother-in-law and others in our circle of family and friends clean and store their empty jelly jars, and carefully wash and freeze their empty eggshells, then tote them to our house as a small, tangible sign of their love and caring.   We receive them as the gift that they are, one that takes sustained effort and demonstrates understanding and support.

Anybody can give a gift from a store. It takes a kindred spirit to give a gift from the heart.

Judi Kotwas

3: IS THE PENNY REALLY THERE?

"I know not how I may seem to others, but to myself I am but a small child wandering upon the vast shores of knowledge, every now and then finding a small, bright pebble to content myself with." - Plato

When shopping for Christmas gifts last year, I found an interesting "coffee table" game that would provide our holiday guests with a pleasant pastime while waiting for appetizers to be served. Described by the manufacturer as "a contained adventure" suitable for ages 8 to 98, the "Find It" game is a sealed, see-through plastic cylinder filled with small, multicolored pellets that look like cross-section slices of toothpicks, along with 47 small items – such as a fishing hook, marble, popcorn kernel, paper clip, button – you get the picture. The object of the game is to find all of the items by spinning, twisting or shaking the cylinder and tallying the viewed items on one of the included checklists.

The game appealed to me because it was self-contained, neat, and seemingly impervious to damage. The sealed design would keep tiny parts from getting lost by child-sized grandchildren fingers, the overall weight guaranteed it would not be batted under or behind furniture by inquisitive young cats, and the cylinder's octagonal end pieces rendered it

roll-off-the-table-and-break-on-the-floor-proof. It
seemed ideal on all counts.

As an added challenge, the manufacturer includes a
penny in each game, and tracks the penny's year with
each game's unique serial number. When the penny
is finally found, the challenge lies in getting it to face
correctly so you can read the year. Then on the
manufacturer's website you input the game serial
number and penny year, and your name is added to
the "I Found The Penny" roster.

When the package arrived, I tried the game myself
before putting it out for guests. It was downright
mesmerizing and hard to put down. While the
premise is simple, the game is more difficult than you
might think. None of my guests could find all of the
objects, let alone the penny. I have played the game
more than anyone else, several hours in total (yes, I
admit it), and have not had even a glimpse of the
penny yet. Although the manufacturer affirms the
inclusion of a penny in every game, I have begun to
doubt its presence. Is the penny really there? I feel
like the man "searching in a dark cellar at midnight
for a black cat that isn't there." (Robert Heinlein)

I can't help but see the parallel between this game and
my own life, where there is something that my five
senses cannot detect although I have the promise of

its truth. Sometimes my faith in my own Manufacturer is too weak. I search for Him in vain, and sometimes lose hope that I will ever be able to read His message for me, or even to find Him. Is the penny really there? Through scripture He has promised He is with each of us, but I sometimes doubt His existence, as undoubtedly others also sometimes doubt.

But what if He designed us purposely to have difficulty finding His "penny" so that we constantly seek and thus stay engaged in Him? Just as the Find It game owes its lasting appeal to the level of difficulty, if we could find our personal "penny," too quickly and too easily, perhaps we would lose interest, move on to another pastime, and lose our focus on the One who keeps us on the right path.

Thank You, dear Lord, for providing enough challenge to keep each of us searching for Your penny in our lives, until that day when we are added to Your "I Found The Penny" roster.

[Author's Note: Two years later, I have not yet found the penny. But I still believe it is in there.]

4: CLUTTER "R" US

"Don't own so much clutter that you will be relieved to see your house catch fire." - Wendell Berry

I just learned that January is National "Get Organized" Month, and that Saturday, January 14, 20012, was National "Organize Your Home" Day.

What OCD person came up with this designation? Organize Your Home DAY? This was obviously meant for those whose possessions are under much tighter control than ours – or anyone I know, for that matter. Can anyone's home truly be completely organized in a mere 24 hours? If your answer is "yes," dear reader, I both envy and congratulate you. Not mine. Not on my best day, with 5-Hour Energy Drink turbo-charging me. I'm not saying that we live in squalor; things are fairly neat at first glance, at least in the rooms within sight of visitors. But please don't wear white gloves, look for your reflection in anything, or open any closet doors or cabinets. Think of it like a tour of the White House; certain rooms are fine to visit - just stay away from the "personal living quarters."

To increase the challenge, my dear husband is a "collector" – he still has the 327 engine from a Camaro that he owned 30-some years ago - and a chaos-lover and creator. Our personal bathroom officially qualifies as a "floordrobe" (a pile of discarded clothes perpetually in a heap on the floor of the room), and none of them are in my size. Our attic seems to provide fertile breeding ground for such things as wire hangers and cardboard boxes - a pair of such objects placed there will magically multiply within a short time. Then there is the basement. And the storage barn (oh, gosh – the BARN…).

My husband's workshop is not even on my list. I know when to hold 'em and when to fold 'em.

Shortly before my early retirement, I made two lists of tasks, one short-term, and one longer-term. My short-term list included the task of inventorying our multiple stacks of stuff so we would at least know what we have and roughly where, donating or selling some, trashing some, and cleaning/organizing/neatly storing the rest. I was certain I could be finished by end of summer, or early autumn at the latest; before Christmas holidays for certain. I started small with the kitchen junk drawer, then the pantry, progressing to bureau drawers and closets. By early summer the house was (somewhat) under control and I began on the attic.

What I failed to factor in, however, is that this task is similar to the stage act where a guy spins multiple plates on multiple sticks, and he has to keep going back to give each plate another push to keep them all spinning, otherwise they wobble to a stop and fall to the floor. You can't organize a junk drawer or closet once, any more than you can eat once and for all. Finally I accepted reality and moved the task to the long-term task list, accepting that it was going to be uphill to get it completed, and constant maintenance to keep things in order.

In the work world, I learned that clutter in a radar system causes serious performance issues, preventing the user from clearly seeing the target. I think it's the same with personal clutter. As Mother Teresa said, "the more you have, the more you are occupied. The less you have, the more free you are." So I'm not going to give up. I'll keep moving our mountain, one shovelful at a time, until one of us is gone.

But I still think they should designate a National Organize Your Home Decade for the rest of us normal slobs.

Judi Kotwas

5: MAGIC AND MIDNIGHT

"If everything seems under control, you're just not going fast enough." - Mario Andretti

When it comes to how people view their vehicles, there seem to be two main camps: Camp #1 is those who see them as merely a means of traveling from point A to point B in the most economical, bother-free fashion. Camp #2 is Car Lover's Camp, for those who like roller coasters, speed, power, and tricked-out rides.

One's choice of vehicle usually reveals the relevant camp. My last four vehicles have been Chevy Camaros, so my membership card reads "Camp #2." There is beauty in nature around us; there is beauty in art, in sweeping architecture, and in the poetry of words. And for me, there is beauty in the exotic lines of a sports car, and music in the low-pitched growl of its well-tuned, powerful engine. I like to get from point A to point B surrounded by a hunk of steel that makes my heart beat a little faster.

Many of us here in Camp #2 actually "humanize' our cars, naming them and thinking of them as 'friends' after a while. One of our campers, Neil Young, wrote a ballad to his cherished first car (named "Mort"), immortalizing its breakdown and reluctant abandonment, and his now-famous song, "Long May

You Run," has become identified with the loss of anything beloved. That's how much Camp #2 members love their cars.

No one really knows why some humans tend to form an emotional attachment to an aerodynamic, powerful hunk of metal. Perhaps it is because, in a society where we feel boxed in by responsibilities and obligations, our cars symbolize freedom, power, and unencumbrance. Or maybe, in their design to be so responsive to their driver's wishes, they appeal to our fascination with technology without diminishing our humanity. All I know for certain is that I have loved sports cars from the time I was old enough to drive.

I bought my first car, an MG-A 2-seater roadster, creamy white with black interior, before I knew how to drive a manual transmission. My father had to drive it home from the used-car lot, my brother's friend taught me how to drive it that afternoon, and that evening I was out cruising in it – wind in my hair, stalling out a lot, but light-headed with joy. I named her "Mystic."

The 1960's ushered in the so-called "pony cars" - Ford Mustang, Chevy Camaro, and Pontiac Firebird. In 1968, I traded in my MG for my first new car, a kelly-green Camaro ("Lucky") with white racing stripes, a white interior, and the best engine Chevrolet ever made – the .327. (I can almost hear the car-lover readers going "Yeah!") The car was a gas-hog, but high-octane gasoline was 35 cents a gallon in those days, so muscle trumped fuel efficiency. I'm not sure the phrase "fuel efficiency" was even used in 1968.

After I moved out of the parents' house and got a dose of real life and real bill paying, the day came when I had to choose between my sweet ride and my own apartment. I chose independence and walking to work over living with my parents again, so the Camaro had to be sold. For some years, finances demanded bus rides and less-than-memorable cars. But that first Camaro had whetted an unquenchable appetite, so in 1983 I bought my next Camaro, black with a gray interior, reminiscent of Kitt, the talking car in the "Knight Rider" TV Series (although Kitt was a Pontiac Firebird); I think a lot of black Camaros and Firebirds were sold that year. I named mine "Shadow."

Magic:
At this point, due to a long commute to work, I was trading in for a new car every four years – always another Camaro. After Shadow came a 1987, yellow with black interior ("Tweety"), then a 1991, dark wine-red with red interior and T-tops ("Wild Cherry"), and finally a 1995, black with black leather interior ("Magic"). In 1996 I joined a vanpool, and

my annual car mileage dropped from about 25,000 to only a few thousand.

Magic already had 28,000 miles on her, but over the next 15 years I added only about 8,000 per year, and formed a deep emotional attachment for this car that I owned for much longer than any before her. She became my silent companion and friend, always delivering me safely to my destination and never once stranding me anywhere beyond help. I loved her to the extent that a human can love an inanimate object, so much so that at about 122,000 miles I spent nearly ten thousand dollars, more than her book value, for an engine rebuild and fresh paint job. She was my Magic. The managers at various repair shops all understood; when they called, they always said "Magic is ready" (instead of "your car is done.")

In April 2011, I retired from the work world and the daily drive, and Magic retired to light duty, mostly short-distance runs for grocery shopping and errands. She and I both suffered signs of middle-aged "deterioration," but she was my inspiration to work through the aches and pains and keep going. Then Magic began needing more frequent repairs as one thing after another wore out, broke or malfunctioned.

Some things, like the leaky valve cover gasket and static-y radio, we just lived with. They were Magic's equivalent of my creaky knees and bad back. Finally, what we thought was a thermostat issue turned out to be a leaking head gasket. (Gasps from the car-lover readers.) Although Magic was still drive-able, without a major repair her time was growing short, and one day soon she would stop running and strand me without warning. The recommended fix was an "engine transplant", to the tune of another six thousand dollars. The less-reliable fix, a new head gasket, would cost $2,500 at least.

I had loved and cared for Magic for all of the years that we had grown old together, but now financial sensibility had to factor into the decision. My husband finally convinced me that it was time to fully retire Magic and get a newer car. I drove her home from the garage on a sunny afternoon, barely able to see through the tears, with Neil's lyrics playing endlessly through my head, speaking to my breaking heart:

> *"We've been through some things together,*
> *With trunks of memories still to come,*
> *We found things to do in stormy weather,*
> *Long may you run;.*
>
> *Long may you run, long may you run,.*
> *Although these changes have come;*
> *With your chrome heart shining in the sun,*
> *Long may you run...".*

We moved Magic to the barnyard and covered her with her custom cover to shield her from the elements while we pondered her final disposition. She was still a pretty car, had served me well, and deserved to be re-purposed rather than just discarded. I knew Magic was an inanimate hunk of metal. I know she had no feelings to be hurt by being replaced. My head knew that she was not really my "friend", but my heart had a mind of its own. I could see her in the barnyard from my kitchen window every day, and the tears still welled up from time to time.

Midnight:

The search began for another car. My husband, knowing my sadness over Magic's plight, encouraged me to "get what I wanted" rather than something practical that would get me from Point A to Point B but that would not satisfy my soul. Well, there WAS a car that I had loved at first sight – the Pontiac Solstice. It was no longer manufactured since Pontiac had gone belly-up, but a used one might just fill the bill. First introduced in 2006, the Solstice was a two-seater convertible with the extroverted, head-turning looks that I love, and the GXP turbo engine option available in 2007, 2008 and 2009 models would provide the satisfying power and speed that car-lovers crave like candy.

I searched the on-line car ads, looking for particular features and exterior colors, and finally came up with "the one" - a 2007 GXP with just over 15,000 miles. Practically new. The only drawback was location – the dealer was almost 200 miles away. I can drive just about any car, but with this one clearing the ground by less than 5 inches, I wasn't sure my creaky joints would be up to the climb into and out of it. Reviews were mainly glowing, but spoke of "falling into" the vehicle rather than climbing into it. We would have to test-drive AND test-fit it before buying. This meant a long drive and the possibility of coming home empty-handed.

From our extensive on-line searching, we knew that this particular car did not remain on the market very long after listing. Apparently "Camp #2" has a large population - this model was being snapped up quickly. We needed a quick decision, or the car would be sold out from under us. So we decided to make the long drive, with the intention of coming back with either the car or the knowledge that we needed a different model car.

Mike arranged his work schedule to get off early one day, and we began the three-hour drive. About an hour into the trip, the salesman called to tell us that another prospective buyer, someone local (and therefore much closer than we were), was on the way in to look at "our" car. We thanked him for the heads-up, provided credit card information to hold the car until we arrived, and counted our lucky stars at the close call.

When we finally arrived at the dealership, we were led to a large building containing several cars in various stages of cleaning and detailing – including "the one." The top was down, and it was a beautiful first sight - navy blue metallic, black leather interior, in seemingly perfect condition. It silently spoke its name to me: "Midnight."

I opened the driver's door, held my breath, and slid in. Painless! Nearly effortless! First hurdle cleared! I put the key in the ignition and started the engine. Its deep-pitched rumbling sang the car-lovers' anthem to us. I climbed back out (almost painlessly! Hurdle #2!) and we put the top up to gauge the difficulty and the visual effect. Still beautiful. After a look under the hood, tire inspection, and other close-up perusal, Mike took the passenger seat and we headed out for a short spin.

I loved the five-speed shift's short throw, perfectly balanced clutch, and ultra- responsive steering and handling. The car was a stranger to me, so at first I was timid with the accelerator. The power seemed adequate, but unimpressive. Then I hit the gas a little more assertively. When the turbo suddenly kicked in, snapping my head back slightly, I could feel an ear-to-ear smile forming on my face. I glanced at my husband, his expression mirroring mine. We pulled off the road and switched seats so he could drive back to the dealer and get his own taste of the candy. He hit it with more confidence and aggression, and the car flattened the mountain road curves. We were both solidly sold, and began the long paperwork process to make Midnight ours.

The process took hours, as car-buying usually does. I sat near one of those big glass car-dealer-type windows and watched the sunlight slowly fade to dusk and then full darkness, knowing what I was facing next - that long, long drive back. I hate driving at night anyway, so I was more than a little nervous at the prospect of a white-knuckle, 3-hour drive home in the pitch-blackness on windy mountain roads, in a beautiful-but-unfamiliar vehicle where all the knobs and controls were unknown to me. It was much more daunting than the half-mile test-drive in broad daylight with my husband sitting next to me. But desire must win out over fear when a beautiful little sports car hangs in the balance.

We were the last customers in the Finance Officer's office that evening. The salesman, manager, and finance officer all shook our hands with one hand while turning off the lights to the place with the other, and we left with a new set of keys and a voluminous bundle of paperwork. Mike drove our old Subaru ("Snowbird") home, while I drove Midnight. I had already located the basics on that short test drive - brake, gas pedal, clutch, gearshift, steering wheel and seat belt - and I was able to find the light switch. All the rest could be figured out later.

Mike drives faster than I do, and he was tired and wanted to get home. We each had cell phones, so when we reached the interstate, knowing I would call if I needed rescuing, he took off, leaving me in the dust. At first I gripped the steering wheel so tightly I believed my hand prints would be permanently embossed into the leather. If I turned to look over my shoulder, all I could see was the back of the seats, not the road. So, terrified and with clenched jaw and stomach, I drove up the ramp onto the interstate and began my solo journey in the right lane, traveling under the speed limit (car-lovers, please stop "boo-ing") and following semi-truck tail lights through the curves in the road, convinced that at any moment I would misjudge a curve and shoot off into the darkness.

Gradually, as the miles went by, Midnight and I became acquainted. By watching cars come up from behind and eventually pass, I learned to gauge my blind spots, and began to trust the views in Midnight's mirrors. Her soft leather seats were comfortable, wrapping around me in a tentative, get-acquainted embrace, and her gauges glowed reassuringly in the darkness, as if to say "trust me, I'll get you home safely." Her road-hugging responsiveness persuaded me to relax into the seat and enjoy the power under my control. I started passing slower vehicles with increasing confidence, and soon was cruising along at five miles over the limit. ((Yes, that's all.) Once in a while, I would goose it, just to hear the turbo say "I'm here." It was intoxicating.

I found my way home alone that night, arriving a half-hour behind Mike, but with a feeling of satisfaction and accomplishment. I had made my first long-distance drive in my new, beautiful little car.

And Magic seemed to approve of her new little sister. Yes, my head knows that cars are just inanimate hunks of metal with no feelings or emotions. But sitting there in our driveway, under a night sky lit by a million stars, with the low rumble from my new little roadster providing background accompaniment, my heart received Magic's permission to go on without her. Midnight would take over from here.

Judi Kotwas

6: ENOUGH LOVE TO GO AROUND

"Love and compassion are necessities, not luxuries. Without them, humanity cannot survive. - Dalai Lama

It is early February 2012. On Groundhog Day last week, Puxsutawney Phil declared six more weeks of winter, and we now face a long stretch with seemingly no excuse for celebration. It is officially the "dead of winter," with leafless trees, hibernating animals, and cold, bare landscapes. The very life force seems subdued and diminished. The majority of us huddle indoors around fireplaces or wood stoves, under afghans and blankets, or swathed in layers of sweaters and socks or warm, cozy robes and slippers.

But wait – right around the corner is the day breathlessly awaited by some, begrudgingly tolerated by others, and torturously painful for still others. Valentine's Day – the day for expressing romantic love with gifts of flowers, candy, and other gifts.

The history of Valentine's Day is a combination of facts and legend. There were several early Christian martyrs named Saint Valentine. The most well-known one, at least in legend, is Valentine of Rome, a bishop who performed secret wedding ceremonies for soldiers in defiance of Roman emperor Claudius II who, believing that emotional attachments made poor soldiers, had banned such marriages. When

Valentine's actions were discovered, he was arrested and thrown into jail. From his subsequent isolation and loneliness, he beseeched his family to write him letters - probably the basis for the first valentine cards. Ah, love.

In today's society, Valentine's Day gifts have extended beyond romantic partners to parents, children and friends. Certainly, Madison Avenue marketers had something to do with this expansion. Valentine's Day has become a major sales revenue stream for florists, confectioners, jewelers and beyond. In 2011, the average American consumer spent just over 125.00 on Valentine's Day gifts, with total retail sales of more than 18 billion dollars. (*BILLION!* I'm guessing there are some diamond necklaces and new cars in there somewhere.)

 Retailers gleefully anticipate the inflow of dollars spent on candy, flowers, jewelry, trinkets, and other symbols of romantic "love". We are bombarded with the not-so-hidden message that if we "truly love" our loved ones, we will buy lots of stuff to give them. Everywhere I go these days, I am confronted with displays of more heart-shaped merchandise than I knew existed. And admittedly, I enjoy flowers and heart-shaped boxes of chocolates as much as anyone else. (Hopefully my husband will read this BEFORE "V-Day"...)

But I can't help but reflect on other aspects of Valentine's Day. As with many other traditions in today's world, it seems that the meaning and purity of the message begins to be eclipsed when commercialized into a nearly unrecognizable retail frenzy.

And what about all those others in our society – those who must walk their paths alone, or who have to choose between heat and food, or those forgotten in nursing homes or asylums, or homeless on the streets? For someone already feeling unloved or forgotten, Valentine's Day can only amplify that sense of isolation and exclusion.

So - should we celebrate Valentine's Day with candy and flowers and romance? Of course! The best relationships need those embellishments to stay on course and at full power.

But why not go further? The very essence of Valentine's Day is about how to best celebrate our love for all those we hold in our hearts. Love exists in many forms – romantic, brotherly, godly – and goes by other names – affection, compassion, friendship, devotion, benevolent concern. Love's most mysterious property is its ability to infinitely expand to encircle each within our chosen group.

I think Valentine's Day reaches its full potential when we honor and exhibit love in all its forms. This

Valentine's Day, find ways to reach out to someone who needs to know they are loved and appreciated. Visit a shut-in, volunteer at a soup kitchen or animal shelter, bake cookies (heart-shaped if you wish) for someone who lives alone. Leave a little bouquet anonymously on somebody's doorstep (ring the bell, run, and watch from the bushes). Give that homeless person a dollar wrapped around a little chocolate heart.

If you are alone this Valentine's Day and feeling bad about it, make yourself a special dinner on the good china and enjoy your own company – you are worth it. Find a way to show that there is enough love to go around, to someone – or even yourself - who has stopped believing it.

Then carry that love into each day of your life. Let that love elevate Valentine's Day above mere rampant commercialism, and transform it into a yearly reminder to let others know, every day, that you see them, and that they matter. Open a door for a stranger. Let the other guy go first at the stop sign. Pay for the guy behind you at the toll booth. Share a kind word and a smile with the tired sales clerk whose feet ache from standing all day. In a society echoing with complaints about the state of the world, choose to help change the state of the world, one random act of kindness at a time. Love has the power, if we

34

provide the mechanism to exercise that power. There is more than enough to go around.

This message was on Facebook today – an essay on Love. The author was not listed. I didn't write it, but I'd like to share it with you:

"*We are all island universes, self-contained points of experience. Within our isolation is safety; in our own minds, we can only hurt ourselves, and even in pain, the self provides a comfortable intimacy. But within that isolation is also desolate loneliness; we need others to be complete. There is no pain greater than connection with other people, and there is no greater joy. Love unlocks that connection. It is the ultimate act of faith, to give yourself over to something entirely out of your control, and to let go. This is where we find love. A power so great it can tear us apart, from cell, to body, to family, to nation. And it binds as well, within couples, families, nations, and beyond. Love transforms, heals, grows; it may be the primal energy of the cosmos, and it unites the self with others, and through them, with the universe.*"

Happy Valentine's Day, with LOVE from me to you.

Judi Kotwas

7: WHY GRANDMAS LIKE TO BAKE STUFF

"We'll order pizza; watch movies too, and do all the things that girls like to do! Like paint our nails and paint our toes, and stay up all night as everyone knows!" - Unknown

Recently, my beloved older granddaughter, Juliana, turned 8. I honestly do not know where eight years went. It is sometimes difficult to remember the years before her, when she was not a vibrant presence in our lives. Most of her birthday parties before this year have been extended-family celebrations with grandparents, aunt, uncle, cousins, neighbors and friends. This year, the plan was for a kids-only, bigger-girl type of party – a sleepover, known in my long-ago youth as a slumber party.

I am a grandma who is quick to volunteer to help out with this type of occasion – perhaps as a subconscious desire to be included and to feel still useful, or perhaps just because I really do like to bake and decorate cakes. My daughter, Jess, and son-in-law, Sean, gladly appointed me captain and sole member of the birthday cake committee.

I began searching for suitably-themed cake decorations, and found plans for adorable slumber-party cupcake toppers, little girls in sleeping bags, that could be adapted to a cake top, with everything

created from "easily obtained" grocery store items.
My plan was to create one for each party guest – 6 all
together – and arrange them on the top of the cake. I
never suspected the learning experience ahead,
although by now life should have taught me to
recognize the signs.

Step one was the shopping list of necessary materials,
which evolved into a scavenger hunt list in the search
for such items as "miniature pink jelly beans" (bought
an entire bag to get the 4 jelly beans needed), purple
and blue fruit chews (eventually gave up and
substituted red and yellow), and small animal-shaped
candies or cookies that would become "stuffed
animals" on the cake (animal crackers were too small
and/or too ferocious; I settled on Teddy Grahams).
Four stores later, I had everything on the list, or
suitable substitutes. I hauled home three grocery
sacks of materials to make one cake. It occurred to
me that there was a marketing opportunity here,
assembling and selling kits with just enough supplies
for one cake. How many others had bought an entire
bag of marshmallows for the 6 needed, or a whole
box of mini-vanilla wafers to use a half-dozen and
eventually toss the rest out when they grew stale on
the cupboard shelf?

I planned to create the cake the evening before the
party, with final touches the next morning right

before delivery. The decorations seemed simple enough; a marshmallow cut in half lengthwise became the body and the pillow. A mini-vanilla wafer for the head, with features and hair piped on with colored icings. Two fruit chews, softened in the microwave for 2-3 seconds and rolled out 1/16" thick, cut into the appropriate sized blanket, trimmed at the top with a small strip from a contrasting color, and decorated with icings and sprinkles before being tucked around the marshmallow body. One or two of the girls with feet (the mini pink jelly beans) hanging out below their blanket. A few with stuffed animals (teddy grahams with piped-on icing faces, and gummy bunnies in pink and blue.) Everything held together with dabs of frosting. How hard could it be? Indeed.

In the pattern for cupcake toppers, the figures were assembled directly onto frosted cupcakes. For the cake, I decided to pre-assemble them on small squares of waxed paper so they could be made ahead and placed on the cake as the last step around the "Happy Birthday" message, It seemed like a good idea at the time.

The cake would go into the oven first, and I would create decorations while it baked and cooled. Juliana wanted half-chocolate and half-yellow cake. No problem. I would use two 9x13 rectangular cake pans, baking one devils food and one yellow cake, then cut each one in half crosswise and stack them, chocolate-on-chocolate, and yellow-on-yellow, creating one 2-layer half-cake in each flavor, then frost the side-by-side half-cakes to create a 2-layer, 2-flavor 9x13 cake. Piece of cake, so to speak.

Granddaughter #2, Bella, was only 3 years old and would not be an "official" slumber party member since she would be put to bed at her usual time in her crib upstairs. Not wanting her to feel left out, I took a little cake batter from the main cakes to make her a cupcake with her own figure and name on it. Jess and Sean also got personalized cupcakes. After all, there was certainly no shortage of supplies for three more figures on three cupcakes.

The cake batters and cupcakes were in the oven in no time. I got out the bags of ingredients and began creating the figures for the cake top., first cutting six small squares of waxed paper on which to build them. The three cupcake figures would be assembled directly onto the iced cupcakes later. I cut the marshmallows, positioned them as bodies and pillows, and added the vanilla wafer heads on the pillows. So far, so good.

The first hint of trouble came with the fruit-chew blankets. After attempting to roll out rock-hard chews after the recommended 2-3 seconds in the microwave, and gooey fruit-chews after 10 seconds, I found through trial and error that 7 seconds was the magic number. Next, I learned that knives, even very sharp ones, do not work well for cutting rolled-out fruit chews into 2x2 inch blankets, let alone the 2x1/2 inch trim strips with the cute scallops shown in the illustration. (I think they used a laser, like one used for those intricate laser-cut paper decorations on greeting cards.) After struggling through a couple of blankets and throwing one away entirely in frustration (ok, I ate it), I switched to small scissors, and also decided to skip the cute, scalloped edges on the blanket trim after cutting a couple of trim strips in half. They would look almost as good if I piped on icing decorations and used various types of decors.

With three blankets made, I decided to tuck them around marshmallow bodies to gauge the effect – and learned that fruit-chew blankets made ahead of time harden back up and don't want to drape over marshmallow bodies without a couple of seconds back in the microwave. And that too long back in the microwave yields a melting, unusable blanket. The next time (if ever) that I make cake toppers of girls in sleeping bags, the blankets will be made out of fondant, not fruit chews.

The next challenge in making the figures came with piping the frostings. I had hair, facial features, blanket decorations, and teddy bear details to pipe. I had also volunteered, in my enthusiasm, to pipe each guest's name on her cake figure. And then there was the "Happy Birthday" cake message. I was working with yellow, blue, green, red, and chocolate frostings. Five frostings, three decorating bags, and one piping tip. Those readers who decorate cakes know what this means. For those who don't, I'll tell you. It means a lot of stopping, emptying one color, washing everything, drying everything, re-loading with a new color. Next lesson learned – the time to create little figures with colored icings is inversely related to the number of icings versus number of piping tips and icing bags. In other words, if it takes 1 hour with 5 icing colors, 5 bags and 5 tips, plan on at least 4 hours with 5 icing colors, 3 bags and 1 tip. I will be buying more bags and more piping tips before the next cake.

After the first figure or two, I learned that piping a name onto a curved blanket, or hair and features onto a tilted vanilla wafer, is more difficult that one might think. I pulled off heads and blankets and began piping on the faces and names before returning heads to pillows and blankets over bodies. I also learned to let the icing dry before positioning anything. Fortunately, smudged features and names can be lifted off with a toothpick and re-done. With the clock ticking away the minutes, I learned that piping eyelashes on little cookie heads late at night just isn't worth the effort. Fortunately, the little girls looked just fine without eyelashes.

By about the 5th figure, I had the technique mastered – sort of. The cupcake figures went quickly and smoothly, thank goodness. When the figures were finally complete, midnight was looming. I decided to keep going rather than risk not having the cake ready on time.

It was time to assemble the cake. It went together according to plan, although the chocolate cake had risen a little more than the yellow and when the two half-cakes were positioned on the board, the chocolate half was a little higher. Fortunately, I could compensate when applying the final frosting that would marry the two halves together into a single cake. Frosting levels the playing field, literally, where cakes are involved.

I had started with three cans of frosting – one chocolate and two vanilla buttercream. (Yes, I used canned frosting.). The chocolate was used between the two chocolate half-cake layers and for some of the piping, and was mostly gone. I had one and one-half cans of vanilla buttercream left, and since Juliana loves blue, I envisioned a blue cake with white clouds floating across it. So I emptied the full can of vanilla buttercream into a bowl, and got out my blue food coloring. I whipped the blue into the buttercream, and the result was – not blue. It was sort of aqua. Not blue. I've never seen an aqua sky with white clouds floating across it. It was late at night, and I had an unfrosted cake and a bowl of aqua buttercream. I could start over, make homemade buttercream and try again to tint it blue, but I would probably just end up with two bowls of aqua buttercream, and lose another hour of sleep.

I began frosting the cake with the aqua icing, covering the four sides before realizing that there would not be enough aqua frosting to cover the top of the cake. Rapidly becoming a master of improvisation, I decided to use the untinted partial can of buttercream to make a white rectangle in the center, in which I would write the birthday message.

Of course, the white frosting did not quite cover, as if an invisible force field created an unbridgeable gap that kept aqua and white edges from meeting. Fortunately, I was not beaten yet. Although it would again involve changing bags and tips, I began piping a rainbow of starbursts, using the leftover yellow, green, blue and red decorator icings, to cover the bare strip around the white rectangle. Not bad. After repeating the rainbow pattern to edge the bottom of the cake, I changed tips one last time, piped on the birthday message, refrigerated the cake, and fell into bed, leaving the final placement of the figures for morning.

The sun rose on the morning of the party. Not one of the six little cake figures would come off its waxed paper backing. With the clock ticking, I placed them, paper and all, on the top of the cake with dabs of frosting, and used small scissors to trim away the excess waxed paper so that it was less noticeable.

After one final chilling, the cake was ready for delivery. Cell phone photos emailed to Jess reassured her that the cake would be there on time. With the original illustration unavailable for comparison, nobody would notice the missing scalloped blanket trims or eyelashes. The white rectangle showcased the birthday message, and the bright colors photographed well. Overall, the cake radiated a cheerful, party mood. I marked the cake board ends with the flavors, and boxed it to be easily slid out at the appropriate time.

Shortly before noon, after a short journey during which my little car found every bump in the road, I delivered the cake, with silent sighs of relief when we uncovered it and found nothing disarranged or broken off. If this cake could take the road bumps, it would hold up to a room full of sugar-charged 8-year-olds. My part was completed. I wished Jess good luck with the party, and went home for a well-earned nap.

The next morning, after sleepy little party guests had been fed a pancake breakfast and were on their way home for naps, Jess called me with the post-party report. It had been a success, including the slumber party birthday cake. The little cake topper figures had been removed intact because of the waxed paper backings - just as "planned"... ☺, and each guest had loved her own personal figure, devouring it completely, which proves that air-hardened marshmallows and fruit chews still taste good when you dress them up enough.

And that's why grandmas like to bake stuff.

8: CAT IS A HAT

"What greater gift than the love of a cat?" - Charles Dickens

As cat lovers will affirm, cats pick their people, and are oblivious to attempts to woo their favor or change their minds. Oh, they can be lured momentarily with treats, but if their "favorite person" is in the vicinity, and if that person is not you, expect to be abandoned as soon as the food is gone.

We have three "rescued" cats in our family: Izzy, our outdoor barn cat, showed up on the back porch one night when extreme hunger overpowered her terror of humans. It took us weeks to earn her trust. She is a beautiful little female with luxuriously thick, plush black fur, big green eyes, and a little white soul patch on her chest. She took up residence in the barns because we had two elderly house cats that could not adapt to the competition of a pretty young girl like Izzy. Our two elderly girls now play in Heaven, but Izzy loves the freedom of the outdoors and would have been miserable confined to the house, so she is the official "barn cat," now about 18 months old and gorgeous.

We had an empty house and still-grieving hearts last July when Joe was brought to us by a friend. She had found him abandoned in the woods, only about six weeks old, starving and distrustful. We took him in without hesitation. He is a brown and white male tabby with enormous hazel eyes, interesting spotted markings, and the longest tail I've ever seen on a cat.

Shortly after adopting Joe, we went to a local shelter to find him a playmate and brought home Zack, a little gray and white male tabby with green eyes, the softest cat-fur imaginable, short legs, a big belly, and all his whiskers licked off by his overly-anxious mother. In only days, Joe and Zack were inseparable, and they grew up together like brothers. They are now almost a year old, both of them big and beautiful. Zack's whiskers all grew back, and he has actually surpassed Joe in weight, although some of that is his belly. They are both already bigger than Izzy.

I am the supplier of food for these three furry family members, although Izzy, the barn cat, supplements her diet with mice, birds, and any other small furry or feathered creature that is foolish enough to pass within range of her awesome hunting prowess. For the two house cats, I am also the cat box shoveler, claw-clipper and groomer, and provider of toys, medicines, and all the accoutrements of house-cat living. They want for nothing.

So, am I the favorite person of these three? Well, I think I am more of a cat person than is my husband

Mike, and if cats thought more like dogs, I might be. But these are cats, and cats pick their people by their own set of rules. They like me, and like to hang out with me during the day, or when they think treats are imminent.

But nighttime is Daddy Time. There is something about Mike that these cats find irresistible. Perhaps he is a "cat whisperer," although he refers to himself as more of a "cat screamer," because he hollers at them when they do bad stuff. But it really seems that in their eyes, he can do no wrong. They flock to him like seagulls to sunbathers with lunch scraps.

At the end of each workday, when his car pulls into the driveway, Izzy the barn cat, who makes only rare appearances at the house during the day, is sitting in front of the house, waiting patiently to greet her Favorite Person. She vocally commands him to come out to the barn and spend time with her. I never thought my biggest competition would be a pretty little brunette with big green eyes, but there it is.

When Mike finishes outside tasks, the most important being Izzy-time, the house cats eagerly await their turn. Joe is timid and waits to be noticed, but Zack steps right up for the attention that is, in his little cat brain, not a privilege, but an inalienable right. After all, this is his Favorite Person. And he doesn't care what form that attention takes, as long as he isn't hurt by it. Mike and Zack have several games that they play, including Cat Twisting, Cat Stretching, Swing Around In a Bag, and one of Mike's current favorites, Cat Is A Hat, in which he drapes Zack over the top of his head and wears him around the house for a short while. On my best day, I couldn't get away with this with Zack; there would be claw marks down the sides of my head and face, unintentionally inflicted in his scramble to escape such foolishness from me. But whatever Favorite Person wants is okay with him.

When Mike settles into his recliner for a little quiet time at the end of the day, Zack and Joe often make an appearance. They both like to find a comfortable place on his legs or chest, to curl up for a little catnap with Favorite Person. Zack, the more enthusiastic one, also likes to march up to Mike's face and give him prolonged nose-to-nose nuzzles, a clear sign of kitty adoration. I get licks on the hand (a cat's way of informing you that you are accepted as his family member), and even an occasional nose-to-nose touch from Zack, but only Favorite Person gets nuzzled.

I truly love cats. I would love to be the Favorite Person of at least one of them, but cats make their own rules. Coercion and threats will not sway them; treats get them for a moment, but as I said before, when the food is gone, the cats are also gone. They can't be reasoned with or persuaded. They pick their people, and that's that. In this household, I am Avis - #2 and trying harder.

Lately, Joe, the timid one, has been hanging out with me more. Maybe he's tired of being cat #3, and is trying to improve his status by joining the Junior Varsity team. I don't care – it's just nice to have a purring, furry presence curled up next to me in the quiet hours.

Mike and Zack playing "Cat Is A Hat"

9: TUBE TALES

"If you're playing a poker game and you look around the table and can't tell who the sucker is, it's you." - Paul Newman

Every April, my husband Mike and I go on vacation for a week, traveling more than 300 miles to an oceanfront tourist town a couple of states away from home. We've been there so many times that we know all the places to visit and all the best restaurants at which to eat. Year after year, we return to the same hotel. We are not creatures of habit, merely victims of the time-share condo industry.

Years ago, when we were newly-weds, a friend told us about a "free weekend" offer in this particular town - a two-night hotel stay with meals included. Well, who says you can't get something for nothing? So we went, agreeing ahead of time that we would politely listen to the sales pitch, then politely say "no, thank you," enjoy our free dinner, sleep in our free hotel bed, and return home having finally, for once in this life, gotten something for nothing.

There were two glaring flaws in our plan; (1) I have nearly no sales resistance, and (2) Mike, who does, was eager to please his bride. In my defense, they made it sound good – after a few years of payments you have a permanently reserved, "nearly-free" yearly vacation, for just the cost of the annual maintenance fee for upkeep, periodic replacement of furniture and appliances, and other hazy incidentals. You are the "owner" of $1/52^{nd}$ of your chosen condo, and approximately $1/5000^{th}$ of the entire building and all its resources. We should have suspected something when, immediately after we finished signing page after page of paperwork, the sales staff uncorked a bottle of champagne, clearly in a celebratory mood. At the time I thought they were congratulating us. Now we know otherwise.

And so began our love/hate relationship with Week 14 of Unit 1011. Every year, rain or shine, neither holidays, nor weddings, nor unplanned illnesses, nor work crises disturbed our cast-in-stone annual vacation week. As the years passed, the "nominal" annual maintenance fee steadily climbed, eventually multiplying five- or six-fold. Currently it rivals the going rate for a comparable oceanfront condo in April, and must be paid right after Christmas so they have our money more than four months in advance. "Nearly free," indeed.

Not that we haven't tried to plan our escape a time or two. We have the choices of using our week, giving it to someone else, or releasing it into the rental pool and equally sharing week 14's rental profits with other owners in the pool. For an additional annual fee, plus more individual transaction fees, we could theoretically trade our week for a week at another location, but exercising this option can quickly become the poster child for the nickel-and-dime concept. Even my gullibility could detect the logic in avoiding that path. One year we decided to release our week into the pool and recoup at least a portion of the annual "maintenance fee." A couple of months past Week 14, we received a check for our portion of the week's rentals - twelve dollars and seventy-five cents. Apparently Week 14 was not in much demand that year.

Next, we tried listing our unit with one of those "sell your timeshare" companies that advertise on TV after receiving an unsolicited offer from them. After the timeshare sales experience, our scam detector should have sounded an alarm, but had been muffled by the desperation to escape. Like trapped animals, we gnawed off our paw of rationality and took the bait. In our defense, the telephone agents were clearly talented actors, with their oh-so-sincere demeanor masterfully played. We were left poorer, wiser, and still in possession of our timeshare week. If anyone reading this has a timeshare and is considering one of these companies - I can say this with total certainty: Don't Do It, It's A Scam. Make a needlepoint sampler of that phrase, hang it over your phone, and just say "No."

This year, as usual, we traveled on the 14th Saturday of the year to Our Place By the Sea. We made the trip more interesting by traveling in a two-seater car with a tiny trunk, requiring us to limit our wardrobe choices and ship some things ahead to the hotel. It was a sort of game to find out how tightly I could pack and how small a wardrobe would suffice, and it helped mitigate the ho-hum aspects of our yearly pilgrimage.

This year, the 14th Saturday fell on the day before Easter, so we missed Easter dinner with family; but as always, our condo awaited our arrival, Unit 1011, reserved for Week 14, for just us. I felt so special.

Upon arrival, we began our stay as always by opening the drapes and walking out onto the balcony, to be greeted by the same familiar, but nonetheless picturesque, ocean view. Inside, new living room furniture stood by to serve us, cleaner but just as uncomfortable and ugly as the old stuff, in colors I wouldn't choose if someone paid me (instead of the other way around). But that ocean view – beautiful and unchanging, and impervious to redecoration or replacement, thank goodness.

We noticed that one feature of the beach, first appearing in 2003 after Hurricane Isabel ravaged the beachfront, was still there as it had been for all the years between: a large, black tube, about 2 feet in diameter. It was in its same location, partially buried in the sand with its exposed end about halfway to the water, facing the sea, with a sort of mini-cliff that elevated the seaward end of the tube about five feet above the sand. I don't recall ever seeing the tube being actually used, but we know it is used to pump sand back onto the beach to rebuild storm-induced erosion. Even after Hurricane Irene swept through last summer, "our" beach remains nice and wide, as it has always been, so the tube must be doing its job. In 2003, I considered it a blemish on the beautiful stretch of sand; now I barely remember the beachfront without it.

One of Mike's few quiet time activities is sitting on the balcony with his dolphin-watching binoculars and looking for dolphins, ships, and interesting beach activity. Early April weather is unpredictable and not always conducive to sunbathing and playing in the ice-cold surf, so this year, with the chilly weather most days, most beach activity centered around individuals of all ages playing on and around the tube, sitting or walking along it, and some daring to jump off the end.

It seemed that people desperate for something to do would settle for the simplest diversion, so the tube's popularity grew as the week wore on, and Mike would come in from the balcony to entertain me with the interesting details. The first day, as he looked out at the ocean, he noticed a young couple playing on the tube. The girl had straddled the tube and shimmied out toward the sea, sitting near the end. The boy grabbed the end of the tube and moved it around, creating the rubber equivalent of a mechanical bull, for a rodeo ride his girlfriend would not soon forget.

Then there were the brother and sister. The girl was about 8 years old, and half the size of her 12-year-old brother, who was attempting to walk the length of the tube. He walked gingerly to about halfway, hesitated, and turned back. We imagined him daring his sweet little sister to go, as my brother would have done with me years ago, and as Mike would have done with his sisters. Big brothers love egging little sisters on. The little girl jumped up on the tube, pranced out to the end, and, as if on a diving board, fearlessly leaped off to the sand below. I'm sure it will be a while before her brother lives it down, especially with at least one binocular-armed witness, and probably many more, on balconies in several buildings.

Mike's favorite was the group of three "tween" aged girls, challenging each other to determine who could go the furthest out on the tube. The first one made it halfway before turning back. The second girl got a little further, but turned back. Finally the third girl, the tallest with noticeably larger feet, made her attempt. She made it out to the end, handed her camera down to the sand where the other two stood, and jumped while the others snapped pictures. Mike would have awarded her the trophy for best tube trip except that she didn't get airborne as the little sister had earlier.

I know my husband. He wanted to take that walk on the tube, too. Sure enough, on the third or fourth day, during our sunset beach walk, Mike gave in to his child-side and gleefully walked the tube himself, jumping off the end and landing in the sand with an ear-to-ear grin. Somebody on the balconies was probably watching him through their dolphin-watching binoculars.

Mike and I have different views of the ideal vacation scenario. I am happy to read, relax, watch TV, and play cards or other games, but Mike craves activity and adventure. Somehow we manage to enjoy our week, alternating active days with quiet time. My sympathy goes out to my dear husband, who is always on the lookout for new solo activities to occupy him during my down time. I resolve to make more effort next year to plan more of his brand of fun so he doesn't have to settle for tube walking to fend off the inevitable boredom of sitting around.

Because the tube will probably still be there, and I've come to the realization that we will, too.

For years to come.

10: TRASH SHOOT

*"The difference between the right word and the
nearly right word is the same as the difference
between lightning and the lightning bug." - Mark
Twain*

When I was a child in elementary school, the ability
to spell was held in high esteem. I can remember
almost winning the sixth grade spelling bee; I came in
second, and the word I missed at the end was
GUARD - I reversed the A and U. It was a lesson
learned, and I have never again misspelled the word
GUARD, for more than fifty years since. I often
recall that near-victory when friends, co-workers and
family members ask for help with spelling. I was just
one little word away from sixth grade championship
glory.

Maybe that's why one of my pet peeves is the ever-
increasing number of spelling errors in TV
announcements and notices, on billboards and signs,
in written advertisements, and even in published
literary works. Perhaps "peeve" is too strong a
description for something that is more a blend of
irritation and amusement. Some of the unintentional
results are very entertaining. I simply find it ironic
that with today's technology providing a world of
information literally in the palms of our hands, one of

the greatest societies in the world appears to be evolving into a nation of spelling-bee losers.

Here's my theory. Somewhere in the 20th century, probably in response to liability lawsuits, manufacturers began to design common sense into products, and lawmakers passed laws mandating usage. This effectively took the intellectual burden off the average citizen, who seemed content to be "taken care of" in a bubble of relative safety. Over time, the ripple extended outward and we became accustomed to letting others do our thinking for us.

In today's perpetually 'plugged-in' society, computer technology has shrunk to take-me-along dimensions in the form of net books, tablets and pads, multi-functional e-readers, and even cell phones that are often "smarter" than some of their users. We are content to rely on these little devices to "take care of" us, to remind us of appointments, navigate to our various destinations, play with us as we wait in lines and reception areas, and provide immediate contact with friends, family and the internet. Some smart phones will even help chase away loneliness, capable of politely holding up their end in a conversation. Perhaps we believe smart phones will take care of our thinking for us, too.

Here we stand, poised on the threshold of a ubiquitous portal of access to virtually limitless information, armed with all the necessary tools to open the door, and we can't seem to find the spell-check key. I am not a fan of virtual keyboards and would love to hang all the blame on them, but the trend extends far beyond cell phone MMS. Spelling errors are in rich supply for anyone on the lookout, and I am on a perpetual blooper hunt. Few days pass without at least one sighting. I find it irritating and unprofessional that a company, a newspaper, or television station permits these errors to slip past the editors and proofreaders.

The fun part is in creating the corresponding mental picture. For example, a recently televised weather report on a prominent channel warned of impending storms, with thunder and LIGHTING. How comforting to know that I wouldn't have to stumble around in the dark trying to get out of the downpour!

When we were on vacation this year, I noticed a myriad of small bloopers in the signs and printed material in our hotel. The prizewinner was on the door of a utility room next to the elevator on our floor. A sign indicated that the room contained waste receptacles for the convenience of guests who don't want to live with overflowing wastebaskets until the next scheduled housekeeping visit. The door was prominently labeled "Trash Shoot." Inside the door was a broom-closet-size cinderblock room, with Rubbermaid-type large covered trash cans. There was no slot or opening anywhere in the wall, so I was a bit confused by the sign. Was this a case of misspelling, or the description of a bizarre disposal method? Admittedly, this tourist town isn't much into recycling or other green practices, but the implication struck me as a rather extreme solution. I envisioned articles of trash flung out like skeet over the twilight ocean, followed by volleys of shotgun fire.

Oh, well. Since I can't change the growing trend single-handedly, I've decided to relax and enjoy the entertainment value. I'm going to begin a journal of spelling bloopers; someday it might provide enough material for a nice book. I've decided to include a separate section containing the made-up words that show up from time to time (when a new car ad uses the description "FLUIDIC styling," what exactly does that mean?)

I'll begin the list right after we get back from the next trash shoot.

11: ANNIVERSARY CAKE

"My path has not been determined. I shall have more experiences and pass many more milestones." - *Agnetha Faltskog*

April 29th, 2012, was the first anniversary of my last day of work before retiring. The time passed stealthily, bringing changes nearly undetectable when viewed from a daily perspective. Yet looking back, the distance covered is evident.

In the beginning, I stood poised in the retirement doorway armed with to-do lists of tasks and projects that had long been postponed due to the hectic workday and long commute, and enthusiastic plans to re-organize, de-clutter and simplify, followed by spending long, golden afternoons in pursuits of my choosing. At first, I felt isolated, struggling to find my stride, like the first time jumping into the double-dutch jump rope game on the school playground so many years ago. There was the twin-slap of the work world going on without me, and of friends near home also going on without me, busy within their own spheres of activity. To integrate myself into a new pattern required stepping out of one bubble into another, standing briefly with a foot in each but belonging to neither.

Life fills whatever time you give it. Energy does not diminish, given more time; it re-channels into fresh outlets of activity. I can look back at the "pre-retirement me" and admire the woman who somehow juggled home and work with at least C+ results, unable to give 100% to either side but managing to stay afloat on both fronts.

I can also appreciate the person I have become since then, emerging from the isolated grotto of reorganization into the warm sunshine of a more serene, softer, brighter world in which there is enough time for small acts of kindness to lighten the load, just a bit, for others. Enough time to have lunch with friends who don't want to eat alone, accompany friends and family to doctor appointments, water plants and tend pets for vacationing acquaintances, run errands for my mother and her nursing-home companions and staff, and shower extra, much-appreciated attention on my dear husband. Enough time. It is a blessing and a source of joy.

Then there is the most recent twist.

With my beloved landscape painting temporarily postponed until completion of the painting cabin in the woods, I discovered cake as a new medium. With no training in classic cake decorating methods, I enjoy the challenge of creating one-of-a-kind cakes and cupcakes using readymade, edible items – cookies, pretzel sticks, fruit chews rolled out into thin, cuttable sheets, marshmallows and a variety of candies, and decorative icings. Rice krispie treats can be carved and shaped into almost anything and will not collapse the most delicate cake texture.

After a few unique cake creations for family and friends, I was dubbed the official "family cake baker." In ten weeks, I have made a slumber party cake, fishing boat cake complete with shark (made out of a Twinkie), cat-lover's birthday cake, woodworking-themed cake with chocolate saw cutting through a rice-krispie-treat plank, marshmallow-orchid-topped cupcakes, and a strawberry-garden cake adorned with red gumdrop strawberries and marshmallow strawberry blossoms. Two future cakes currently on the drawing board are a musical-theatre cake and a replica of Van Gogh's "Starry Night." I know this is an election year, but I draw the line at a cake replica of the White House.

I am no competition for the "Ace of Cakes" (Duff Goldman, Food Network star), who could easily build that cake replica of the White House. But each of my cake creations was well-received, with suggestions to start a cake decorating business. Ego-boosting, but a biased audience, after all. Paying customers tend to be a bit more demanding.

Then there is the fact that cake decorating seems to bring out the Mr. Hyde in me, revealing a grouchy old woman who stresses over the details and develops anxiety throughout the effort, before finally basking in the eventual glow of at least partial success. My dear husband has learned that to mess with me can result in claw marks or icing in the hair, so he wisely steers clear of the kitchen during the marathon decorating sessions.

So I question the wisdom of embarking on a business venture that would result in a lower hourly wage than I made when babysitting as a teenager. Labors of love are more enjoyable and gratifying, and I'd like to stay married.

Looking back, I have to conclude that it was a good first year. I'm looking forward to what comes next. I might even bake myself a little cake to celebrate.

12: PAYING IT FORWARD

"My religion is very simple. My religion is kindness." - Dalai Lama

A few years ago, I saw a movie that left a lasting impression. It was about a seventh-grade boy who, given a social studies assignment to create a mechanism to change the world for the better, designed a plan to create a branching tree of selfless acts of kindness. He began the process by selecting three people and performing favors for them; then each recipient, rather than paying back the favor, passed it on to a third person. In theory, the tree of good deeds would rapidly expand, with the potential to change the world. The boy called his plan "Pay It Forward."

The movie heightened my awareness of the world around me and caused me to begin looking for opportunities for random acts of kindness. I have found that a kindness performed anonymously bring me the most satisfaction and reward.

Recently, I was reminded of how it feels to be on the receiving end of unexpected kindness, through a small but significant gesture that meant everything to me.

My favorite entertainer is a charismatic young musician and performer named Adam Lambert. I love his considerable talent, and also his character and personality. His stage presence is gigantic and mesmerizing, contrasting with his off-stage persona – soft-spoken, thoughtful, humble and generous. He must know how his fans cherish him, yet through his music he reveals vulnerability and uncertainty. He is patient with the imposed intimacy of interacting with his fans, seeming to live by the "pay it forward" philosophy.

So when he was scheduled to perform at a venue within driving distance, I rounded up a few friends, and four of us, all ardent Adam Lambert fans, were looking forward to seeing him perform from our fourth-row seats.

We arrived in town early on the day of the show. The youngest and most enthusiastic of our group was 16-year-old Brian. By 3:00 in the afternoon, he was eager to get to the theater and check out the layout for possible celebrity sightings. We found the back of the theater, and Brian joined a small group of fans with ears pressed to the loading dock door, listening to the sound check taking place on stage. One of my friends, Wendy, accompanied Brian, while Kathy and I remained in the van, parking in a back lot about 20 feet away from the theater, with an unobstructed view of the stage door.

Suddenly the stage door opened, and a security guard stepped out – followed by Adam. For just a split-second, the rest of the world blurred away and he was all I could see. He was dressed casually in jeans and a plaid shirt open over a tee shirt, but still he stood out – tall and handsome, sunlight reflecting in the blond accents in his jet-black hair. It was as if an "Adam Force Field" had reached out and touched me. I could easily have rolled the window down, caught his eye, and called out to him. He would have smiled and waved, I am certain. Instead, I sat quietly and watched him walk away, tears welling up and spilling over from the simple joy of his unexpected momentary proximity.

Adam walked quickly to the bus, not pausing to sign autographs, but smiling and speaking briefly to the fans standing nearby – fans that included Brian and Wendy. The excitement was palpable from across the lot as he said to them: "Hi, guys. Are you excited for the show?"

After that, Brian was immovably glued to the spot, fiercely determined to do everything in his power to meet Adam. So Kathy, Wendy and I left him there and returned to the hotel to dress in our concert finery.

A short while later, as we were in the midst of our primping, curling, fluffing and general glamorization, the day took a surreal turn when my cell phone rang and I answered it. It was Brian, so excited he was nearly incoherent. What I heard was: "Adam's here, with me! He wants to talk to you!" Then, Adam's voice: "Hi, Judi". I somehow managed to say "Hi" back, and then he was gone.

Two thoughts immediately struck me:

1. What a wonderful, caring person Adam was, to take time in the pre-show imminent meet-and-greet preparations and chaos, to please his fans in any way he can – even a quick phone hello to someone like me.

2. What a wonderful, caring person Brian Bailone was, to take time, in the excitement, thrill and mayhem of meeting one of his favorite performers, to think of his friend back at the hotel, to make the phone call, and to persuade Adam to say hello, knowing how much it would mean to me. He had also gotten me a personalized autograph, now framed and in a place of honor in my den, to be cherished for the rest of my days.

Brian called back a few minutes later, urging us to hurry back, certain that we would be able to meet Adam when he returned from the meet-and-greet reception in a nearby hotel. We hurried to finish dressing, rushed back to the theater (hitting every traffic signal red, of course), and Wendy and I ran the last three blocks to where Brian waited, while Kathy parked the van.

The crowd of fans around the bus had grown considerably, and security personnel were kept busy creating a clear area. We could see the hotel entrance from a respectful distance back as more and more excited fans pushed in front of us. Soon we saw Adam emerge, but Security hustled him across the street quickly and into the theater through another door, away from the crowd.

With a few hours remaining before show time, we returned to the van. Brian gave me the CD booklet that Adam had signed "For Judy". All over again, I was in awe of Brian's thoughtfulness. Brian had told Adam that we would be in the fourth row, and Adam had told him he would look for us. (Yes, I know he probably says that to everyone.) So we decided to make signs for the concert, knowing that Adam would probably see them. I wanted to somehow thank him for the phone call without gushing like a star struck teenager. When I was finished, my sign was two-sided, reading **FAN LOVE 2 U,** and on the flip side **"HI BACK" FROM JUDI.**

Three acts preceded Adam and his band. When he finally took the stage, it was nearly 10 p.m. The theater nearly exploded with the surge of energy flowing to and from the stage like two-way bolts of lightning. The fan love was palpable, and Adam, his band and backup singers seemed to be genuinely enjoying themselves.

As always, Adam transported the audience through his performance to that higher, happier place that his fans crave like candy. As he performed his final number, he looked our way. Brian is nearly a foot taller than me, and easily stands out in a crowd. He held my "Hi Back" sign up high, and pointed down at me standing next to him (I am short and easily lost in a crowd). A short while later, as Adam began to walk off the stage, he blew kisses to the audience, at least one in our general direction, and waved, giving a smaller wave definitely in our direction. Brian knew that he had seen our sign, and was convinced he was waving at us. And maybe he was. The mere possibility gave me a little jolt of happiness.

After the show, Brian wanted to hang out near the bus, to possibly see Adam again and give me one more chance to meet him. When we got there, the crowd was huge. Security herded people back, and the general scene was chaotic.

It didn't feel right to me. I wanted to tell the crowd to leave Adam alone, to let him rest and re-charge.

Instead, I stood in that crowd with Brian and Wendy for a while, until it became apparent that Adam was either waiting us out inside the theater, or more likely, that he had already been hustled away before the crowd could assemble. We decided to return to the hotel.

I would have loved to meet Adam Lambert, to shake his hand and thank him, but the time was not right yet. It would have to be another time and place. But I had the echo of Adam's voice on constant replay in my head, and a cozy, sweet memory of two special guys who paid it forward to me when I least expected it.

Thank you, Adam. Thank you, Brian.

My two special guys, Brian and Adam

Judi Kotwas

13: GOODBYE, OLD FRIEND

"When there are lines upon my face from a lifetime of smiles, when the time comes to embrace for one long last while, we can laugh about how time really flies, we won't say goodbye because true love never dies. You'll always be beautiful in my eyes." - Anonymous

I live by my emotions, and I love cars. I am therefore preprogrammed to pick a vehicle for the heart-beats-faster element, to name my vehicles, and to become attached to them, humanizing them into "friends" - all a bit strange, perhaps, but harmless enough.

The difficulty arises when the time comes to part with one vehicle and move on to the next. In the past, there was no opportunity for a long goodbye. The end of ownership came like ripping off a bandage; a car was traded at a dealership for a newer one, and although I always felt the quick, sharp pang of separation, the retired vehicle was out of sight, and I could fantasize that it had moved on to "a better life" and walk away from the old and toward the new.

This time is different.

Nearly 18 years ago, on November 30, 1994, I bought Magic, a beautiful little 1995 black Camaro with leather interior. The first time I sat in her for a test drive, she wrapped herself around me in a warm hug, and I loved her from the first moment. Magic was the sixth in a long line of Camaros that I owned, and she was the best and my favorite of all of them. Over the years, she got me through bad weather and long trips safely, and I rewarded her with the best oil and highest-grade gasoline, regular maintenance and detailing, an engine rebuild and new paint job when she was 14 (an illogical financial decision), and my constant devotion. We grew old together.

A few months back, Magic developed the automotive equivalent of a human aneurysm – a leaking head gasket. As any gear head knows, do-it-yourself head gasket replacement is not a major financial endeavor, but is labor intensive and does involve lifting the engine from the chassis, especially in a Camaro, where half the engine is nestled under the dashboard. If, however, your garage is not equipped with a lift, paying someone else to do the labor runs close to three thousand.

Even I was bright enough to realize that investing three thousand into an 18-year-old car was probably not the wisest financial decision. So after a tearful drive home from the repair shop, the decision was made to shop for a replacement vehicle. I found one, a sweet little 2007 navy blue Pontiac Solstice convertible. I named her Midnight, and she took up residence in the garage, taking over Magic's duties.

Meanwhile, Magic rested quietly in the barnyard down the hill, behind the big bank barn, in full view of my kitchen window. For months, she was there to greet me each day as I stood at the sink doing various tasks. Sometimes I walked down, pulled off her cover and sat in her driver's seat, talking to her about old times, and chasing away the ants and spiders who viewed her as a potential new condo. We kept Magic on the car insurance policy until we could decide her ultimate fate. I didn't want her to rust away in the barnyard – she was still beautiful, although ailing – but my heart kept delaying the decision and action.

June arrived, and Magic's annual state inspection was due. I decided to have it done, and take further action based on the outcome. When it was time to take her to the inspection appointment, she started right up on the first turn of the key, seemingly eager to be back on the road, even for a brief outing.

During the inspection, I sat in the waiting room like a parent in a pediatrician's office, waiting to find out my child's health. And she did not fail me this last time. She passed. My little old girl made it through, and I felt irrationally proud of her, as if my child had gotten all A's on her report card.

And I faced the fact that she didn't deserve to rust away in a barnyard. She was built to run the roads. It was time to polish her up and look for a buyer who could do the work needed to give Magic a chance for a few more serviceable years. It was time to say goodbye.

Today, my task is to scrub her up, inside and out, and take pictures for an on-line listing.

I'm delaying again, writing this tale instead of getting out the bucket, sponges, chamois and scrub brush, Windex, Armor-All, tire black and carnauba, but soon I'll be ready to do it. I just need a minute. Magic has been a good car and a good friend. I'll miss the sight of her in the barnyard.

But it's time.

[Author's note: Midnight was sold a few weeks later to a young man, a fellow gear-head, who was able to repair the head gasket himself and get her back on the road, where she belonged. To my knowledge, he is still driving her today.]

14: RAINBOW WATCH

"Walk on a rainbow trail; walk on a trail of song, and all about you will be beauty. There is a way out of every dark mist, over a rainbow trail." - Navajo Blessing

The weather during this summer of 2012 has been unusual, more extreme than typical. The summer has been, as anticipated after an unusually mild winter, very hot with an overabundance of insects in the garden, and a lot of turbulent storms. The good news is that there has also been a higher incidence of rainbows.

I love rainbows. I have always been mesmerized by the sight of a rainbow softly glowing against the backdrop of dark clouds after a rainstorm, and because of God-fearing parents and diligent Sunday school teachers, I've always viewed a rainbow as a comment and sign of reassurance from God. Time after time, when facing a tough situation in my life, I have looked to the skies, searching for a rainbow, my own personal God-speak for "you're going to be all right, I promise."

The scientific explanation of a rainbow is uncomplicated – a simple spectrum of light that appears in the sky when the sun shines on droplets of moisture in the atmosphere, taking the form of a multicolored arc. Yet, despite the scientific simplicity of its genesis, a rainbow whispers its aura of surprise and mystery to our deeper, spiritual selves, and remains an endlessly explored topic of poets and artists. Geometrically perfect and all the more precious by virtue of its spontaneous brevity, the rainbow stops people in the tracks of their daily routines to gaze for a moment at its ethereal perfection. I don't think I know anybody who doesn't like rainbows.

There have been years when I saw no rainbows at all. Most years, I see at least one or two. The most spectacular one during our years on the farm came on a summer afternoon when I was home alone. It was a rare double rainbow, with the faintest suggestion of a third bow, arched in perfect visual composition over a big, beautiful maple tree behind the big bank barn. Did you ever notice that in a double rainbow, the colors on the second bow are in reverse order from the first one? I had no camera to capture that postcard-perfect image, but I still remember its breathtaking beauty.

This half-spent summer has treated us already with multiple rainbows. I would have missed the most recent one were it not for the thoughtfulness of some nearby neighbors who live up the hill from our little farm. As we like to say, we are their scenic view. From their viewpoint, most rainbows appear in the sky right over our house, and on this occasion they called to tell us that we were once again in that celestial frame. I rushed outside, still on the phone expressing my thanks for the call, in time to see the familiar, beloved sight before it faded away.

A few years ago, in a moment of deep despair, I prayed for the impossible – I asked God for a rainbow, as a sign that He was with me and that things would work out. It was a bright autumn day, late in the afternoon. The sun was shining and the skies were blue and clear with just a few fluffy, white clouds. I looked into the sky above the big barn, where rainbows normally appear after a rainstorm.

When the rainbow appeared, blinking on like a just-energized fluorescent light, and off again just a few seconds later, it was a life-changing moment. Some would say my imagination was active that day, but I know what I saw.

Scientifically, it was not impossible. It just required enough droplets of moisture in the atmosphere, with just the right angle of sunlight to reflect through them, at just the moment that I needed to see it, in exactly the part of the sky before me. That's all. Ever since then, I have regarded rainbows with additional reverence and joy.

In my life, I've had answers to impossible prayers, both big and small. I've had help when I thought there was none, and grace when I least deserved it. It is nearly incomprehensible that a universal force would reach down, among the billions of people on this planet, which is itself one out of countless in the universe, to provide divine assistance to one tiny point of humanity; but it happens, again and again, too often to be attributed to coincidence. So I'm more careful these days to look for the small blessings even in tough situations, and to give thanks for each one, and credit where credit is due.

Recent scientific research has revealed that when a human is in a meditative state, communicating with his Creator, by whatever name he chooses, a specific area of the brain "lights up" with activity, as if within the hidden depths of untapped mental capacity there is a special section designed in to facilitate that unique communication. I believe it. And I believe that there is a force greater than ourselves at work in the universe and on this big, blue marble we call Earth. Call it what you will – God, Jehovah, Allah, Yahweh, Mother Nature, the Great Force, or whatever. It's out there, and for whatever reason, it wants to connect with its human creations. There are signs, if we remain receptive to them.

One of my signs is a rainbow. I'm always watching for the next one.

Judi Kotwas

15: HAPPY EVERYTHING

"Time for work - yet take much holiday for art's and friendship's sake." - George James De Wilde

One of my hobbies is embroidery, and I have several projects queued up for "whenever I get to them." But recently, leafing through one of my favorite needlework catalogs, I saw a needlework kit that compelled me to buy it and bump everything else in the queue to work on this one first.

It is simply a sign that covers all of the holidays in the year in chronological order, proclaiming "Happy Everything", with appropriate graphics of the holidays interwoven around and between the letters, beginning with the winter of a new year around the "H" of Happy, and culminating with Christmas at the other end. What a great concept!

People love holidays, for a lot of reasons. While it is true that some holidays bring sadness, loneliness, or anger and resentment; most people have at least one that they eagerly await, if only for the break in the daily routine - time off from work and the opportunity to sleep late, catch up on household projects, or have leisure time alone or with friends and family.

The earliest holidays were religious in nature; the word itself comes from the words "holy day". In today's world, holidays take many forms. In addition to religious holidays, we have national holidays, ethnic holidays, holidays established to motivate people into action, and smaller, personal holidays of appreciation and celebration that draw family and friends closer together. Some holidays are days of festivity or recreation when no work is done.

Holidays give us anticipatory pleasure on dark, dreary winter days, relief from the stress and chaos of daily routine, the opportunity to honor someone special within our world or our smaller circle, and the pleasure of our own day to feel special. Holidays bring special treats, green beer, and a legitimate excuse for chocolate. Through holidays, we reinforce family tradition and relive childhood memories. Holidays are more about looking back than forward, with rituals of reassurance.

Holidays tend to condense their essence into the highest highs or the lowest lows. Sometimes we set ourselves up for disappointment, pinning too much expectation on holidays, especially the family-centered ones, like Thanksgiving and Christmas. Sometimes we get caught up in the decorating, shopping, traveling, cooking, and such. Sometimes we fall into a pattern of going through the motions, spending too much money, and not enough heart, losing sight of the essential purpose for all our efforts. But we have the power to take back our holidays, pause in the frenzy of preparation and planning, and remember each holiday for what it really is.

I'd like to add one more, central holiday, "Happy Everything" Day. Those grinches who want to get the holidays over and done with could then be off the hook for a whole year. The rest of us, who would still celebrate all the others, would have one more special day added to our calendars.

We could hold it on the 183rd day of the year, the exact halfway point, July 2. We could celebrate with champagne and noisemakers, flowers and candy, corned beef, jellybeans and Peeps, burgers on the grill and potato salad, a big turkey with pumpkin pie, and decorated cookies (oh, the possibilities THERE!).

Our parents could be the guests of honor, with special seating near our beautifully decorated tree - hearts, shamrocks, little flags, and tiny ghosts and witches nestled among the traditional glass balls and twinkling lights.

At the end of the day, while watching fireworks in the twilight sky, we could reflect on the importance of love and friendship, of sacrifice and selfless bravery, and the events and heroes and helping hands that got us where we are today, collectively and as individuals.

And if we are really, really smart about this, we could carry that sense of joy and appreciation into every day of the year. We could let it transform us, helping us rediscover our best selves as we interact with the people and the world around us, sharing the spirit of "Happy Everything" with each word, each smile, and each random act of kindness.

I'm already working on my sign for it.

16: IT'S A JUNGLE OUT THERE

"You can't just wade in with a weed whacker; you don't know where the plant stems are." – Walter Murch

A few days ago, I got myself momentarily lost, a common occurrence since I am one of the 'geographically challenged.' What made this time different was that I was in my own yard.

During the course of these summer months, our large vegetable garden has metamorphosed into a verdant entity, a gargantuan, waist-high, leafy green sea bisected by the Great Wall of Sunflowers, inhabited by an insect population steadily growing in both size and variety. It is reminiscent of what Jack discovered at the top of the beanstalk - a world in which everything towered above him in large-scale splendor.

The sunflowers reach skyward several feet above my head, with blossoms larger than industrial pizza pans. Squash and zucchini plants boast elephant-ear leaves with yellow and green offspring that mature at an astonishing rate from finger-sized to produce-stand-readiness.

Luxurious tomato plants spill over their stakes and supports in decadent abundance, far surpassing their anticipated sizes. All of the crops, in fact, have exceeded our dimensional expectations, and have all but obliterated most of the space between rows.

To traverse the garden we must take complicated, twisting paths through their mysterious labyrinths. I absent-mindedly took a false turn one day, and ended up dead-ended between the sunflowers and the cantaloupe patch, unsure of how to extricate myself without trampling any of the adolescent melons, or breaking fragile tomato plant branches behind me. Lost in the jungle! The narrow paths begrudgingly permitted by the rapidly expanding leafy inhabitants of our garden tend to be one-way routes because of plant configurations and the delicate fragility of branches laden with ripening produce.

All of this growth caught us by surprise this year. Soil tests at the beginning of planting season indicated general depletion in all of the vital elements, so Mike worked the plot, tilling in his own custom mix of composts, barn hay, and other good nutrients. Based on the record growth we are seeing, maybe he's onto something… I hope he wrote down the secret formula.

The weeds certainly appreciated the extra nutrients, growing vigorously, rapidly, and relentlessly. In some locations, they are nearly machete-worthy, although our usual dispatch methods are weed whacker, lawn mower, or barehanded yanking (the most satisfying one-on-one method, man versus weed). One thing we have learned about weeds – they don't ever take a day off, and in the battle for garden dominance, we'd better not, either. The weeds lie in wait for just such an advantage.

So maybe Mike's special nutrient blend can be credited with the extraordinary plant growth this year, both cultivated crop and weed. But it doesn't explain the insect population explosion. I have seen insects this year that I've never seen before in my life. There are new varieties of wasps and beetles, bugs that I can't even relate to a type (is it a beetle or a spider? Looks like a hybrid of both...) and more quantity and variety of ants than we've had in past years. I think last year's unusually mild winter gave them all a buggy boost - nobody in the herd got killed off by the cold (what cold?), and everybody in the herd woke when the alarm went off early, in March instead of May. By the time gardens were planted in April, the bugs were already waiting in the wings, so to speak. Anyway, that's my theory. All I know for certain is that all of the insects appeared very early in the season and are proving to be worthy opponents in this year's garden wars.

Their activity level is higher, too. In the strawberry beds, countless whiteflies rise in an irritating cloud whenever the plants are disturbed, like the cloud of dust that perpetually surrounds Charlie Brown's endearingly grimy friend, Pigpen, from the Charles

Schultz "Peanuts" comic strip. The ants swarm over human hands trying to pick berries and bite their annoyance at being disturbed and having "their" berries taken away. (The least they could do is pull a weed or two to earn those berries.)

Wasps are building nests in new and different locations, like the one we discovered a few days ago. Mike uses those orange plastic cones in locations in the yard and garden to mark obstacles and objects that could potentially damage a weed whacker, tiller, lawn mower, or unsuspecting foot or ankle. One cone marks a hose near the farthest-out strawberry bed, and when Mike happened to glance down when passing close to it, he discovered a cluster of wasps feverishly creating a new nest just inside the tip of the cone. Wouldn't THAT have been an unhappy surprise if he had moved the cone without looking…

Then there are the bees. According to the local hive keeper who supplies us with honey for our produce stand, the bees began honey production earlier than usual this year, and finished earlier to begin swarming. This resulted in a reduced supply of local honey, and unusually grumpy bees. I'm no bee expert, so I'm not sure of the correlation. I can tell you that they are much less tolerant of my presence in the raspberry patch, frequently flying up in front of my nose as if to shake a little bee-fist in my face to warn me off. I have already been stung twice this season, as much as in several preceding years put together, and undeservedly in my opinion, although I still feel a pang of regret when seeing a tiny, lifeless bee body hit the ground after bravely sacrificing to defend against a perceived but non-existent threat.

The overall bee-to-human spirit of peaceful coexistence is perturbed this year, although there is a glimmer of hope for détente. This morning, in the early morning hours, I accidentally touched a bee that was resting on a raspberry leaf before beginning his long day's work. My finger barely stroked him, almost like gently petting a beloved cat, and he remained resting quietly. I backed away on tiptoe, breathing a sigh of relief

As in every summer's garden wars, some of our skirmishes with the pests and diseases have not been successful. We recently conceded the green beans to the bean beetles after all of the plant leaves had been reduced to delicate green lace that struggled to sustain life before finally succumbing. Mike removed the skeletal remains from their rows and tenderly tucked them into the compost heap.

The strawberry beds fell to the ants, slugs, and millions of whiteflies. Next year we will move strawberries to a new location and begin with all new plants and new, ant-free soil. The cucumbers started off well, but then yellowed and withered on the trellises. We aren't sure what killed them - possibly cutworms. We will collar the vines next year and see what happens.

Fortunately, the satisfaction of garden victories continues to exceed the occasional pangs of defeat. Lettuce, radishes and carrots grew well in their new location. Blueberries, now finished for the season, were plentiful and delicious. Squash and zucchini are in their third month of production. Red and white potatoes emerge from the soil in picture-perfect form. Raspberries are abundant and enormous. Early tomato plantings did not look promising, so Mike put in more plants. All survived, resulting in several dozen huge plants now heavy with the weight of ripening tomatoes of several varieties that promise a bumper crop in the next few weeks.

The first patch of corn was the sweetest ever, and the second patch is ready for harvest. Mike has spotted groundhogs circling patch#2 like furry brown vultures, but he has plans for them. You may remember from my first book, "Life On The Farm - Out To Pasture," that he is The Dragon Slayer. Those groundhogs should be saying their prayers, writing their wills, and kissing their wives goodbye. The critter chart is back up on the refrigerator door, ready for updates.

Our summer days, early mornings, and evenings tend to center around work in the garden, a source of happiness and satisfaction, a means of healthy exercise, and a daily battleground with the weeds, insects, birds and other predators. Some days we win. Other days, they do. We arm ourselves with a mini-library of organic gardening books and frequent Internet searches for helpful information. Organic gardening requires planning, thought and effort to find ways to feed the plants and defeat the predators without chemicals. We stay committed to working the earth without harming the earth, and to raise produce that nourishes without harming ourselves.

We hope we are slowly taking control of our garden domain, and gardening a little smarter each year. It's a jungle out there, particularly this year. But it's our jungle.

Maybe we should attach vines to the sunflower plants.

Judi Kotwas

17: SEE GRANDMA SKATE

"I have recently taken up two new sports: roller skating and ankle spraining, in that order. I am getting quite good at both." - Miles Kington

A very long time ago, when I was young and all of my joints were limber and problem-free, I was a pretty good skating rink roller skater. I took lessons, and was able to "dance on skates", with backward skating, jumps (little ones), and couples' skating maneuvers similar to figure skating on ice.

There were no in-line skates then, just above the ankle, lace-up boots with 4 wheels attached, now known as "quads." We wore those cute little skating skirts, essentially just briefs with a little material surrounding them, that left legs totally unencumbered for complete freedom of movement, and totally unprotected in the event of falls or tumbles. Kneepads and helmets had not yet been adopted as skating safety equipment, so the evidence of the learning process was revealed in skinned knees, abraded elbows, and a colorful array of bruises.

The last time I went skating at a rink, my daughter was a teenager and I was the church youth group leader. I was doing fairly well after a shaky start relearning my balance on four wheels with no built-in brakes, navigating the oval track and feeling somewhat confident, until I crashed into another skater. As he tried to help me up, I slipped again and pulled him down to the floor. The girls in the youth group later teased me mercilessly, convinced I had deliberately staged the collision with the cutest guy in the place. Was he? I was far too mortified and humiliated to notice. The day after that, my back, hips and knees shouted a relentless, nonstop chorus of "you are no longer that teenager who could dance on skates."

Today, I am "Grandma" to two precious granddaughters – Juliana, 8 years old, and Isabella, who will be 4 in October. Juliana has invited me to her skating party at a nearby skating rink, and now I have some serious thinking to do. Two roads diverge in the yellow wood just ahead, and I have to decide which path to take.

Should I exercise the "Grandma Option" that permits me to sit safely on the sidelines and watch the action, cheering my granddaughter on with every lap? I could guard purses and street shoes; I could helpfully keep an eye on the younger children; I could fetch drinks and snacks for the skaters. A grandma is a valuable asset at a skating party, after all.

Or should I choose to be "G-Ma", the coolest grandmother in south central Pennsylvania? I could rent me a pair of those "quads", lace them on, and hit the rink. I could seek to recapture a snapshot moment of my glory days – at a price, of course. I would need to spend the next day with my newest friends: Ben Gay, Cele Brex, "Jets" (bathtub feature), and Mr. Pad, as in Heating. My first inclination is to go the conservative route, particularly in light of on-going diagnostic tests to find the cause of hip and back pain severe enough to cause a noticeable limp.

The day of Juliana's skating party is here. At the rink, the bustle of activity begins as the kids and many of the parents exchange street shoes for rental skates. There are a few spectators like me, remaining seated or leaning against the walls surrounding the rink floor, taking pictures and smiling at the excited chatter all around them. Intellectually, I know they are the smart ones. I take my place among them and begin snapping pictures of my granddaughters, daughter and son-in-law, smiling and waving like a well-behaved grandma.

But the younger me, still alive and ready for adventures, pleads to come out to play. Soon I can feel "G-Ma" struggling to break free from good old grandma. She will not be ignored. I stand up, saying "I'm going to try it!" and before I can chicken out, trade my shoes for ugly, light brown shoe skates with orange wheels and laces – a far cry from the beautiful, glove-soft white leather pair I had owned in younger days. I test the amount of "roll" in the wheels; nothing would be more humiliating than falling down just trying to stand up. I loosen the laces, step into the skates – they feel like familiar old friends - and tie them securely. I slowly rise to my feet, which mercifully remain in alignment with the rest of me rather than shooting out in opposite directions and dumping me onto the floor. So far, so good! Nobody is impressed; nobody even notices, I'm sure – except my daughter, smiling her approval, and my granddaughter, who is thrilled to see grandma on skates like everybody else.

It would be nice to say that it all came back and I floated around the rink effortlessly. It would also be totally untrue. I make my way slowly, tentatively, and close to walls and other handholds, careful not to wrench protesting muscles and joints, with a new appreciation for anyone who overcomes any sort of adversity to relearn a lost ability. I am learning to skate all over again, with a changed sense of balance, a body that is aerodynamically different, and joints that no longer move as they once did.

There is no major victory this afternoon, but to try at all is a small triumph and a lot of fun. The experience is both humbling and exhilarating. I am reminded that I am not as young as I would like to be, but not as old as I fear. I don't fall, not even once. It is an adventure!

After skating, I join my daughter and her family for dinner at a nearby restaurant before driving home. Juliana rides with me to the restaurant in my little 2-seater convertible that she refers to as "Grandma's Sweet Ride," under a sky filled with clouds and low rumbles of thunder signaling the imminent threat of rain. We need a little more adventure today, and decide to put the top down for the trip. When we arrive at the restaurant ahead of the rain, pause to put the top up, and smile as we watch the downpour during dinner. Another triumph!

There will be a price to pay tomorrow. It will be worth it.

18: THE JOURNEY OF LIFE

"And in the end, it's not the years in your life that count. It's the life in your years." - Abraham Lincoln

On a recent morning in August, while standing in the midst of tomato vines that have escaped their restraints and spill joyfully over the ground in a waist-high leafy green sea, I was struck by the similarity of the search for the ripe, beautiful red globes, many hidden from view beneath the luxuriant green canopy, and long-ago childhood Easter egg hunts. So many snapshot memories of those early years draw parallels to present day activities, like training exercises costumed as childhood games, preparation for the bigger, all-important one barely glimpsed on the horizon - the Game of Life, scarcely begun.

With humans, as with many animal species populating this big, blue marble of Earth, youthful play is a mechanism for learning life skills that facilitate successful navigation of life's course and its many challenges. As a toddler, I began mobility with brute force, having not yet learned that I could dial down the intensity on my actions. I crashed into tables, broke crayons, tore pages from books, and watched in confusion as beloved cats or dogs ran for safety from my "petting" attempts.

But then, childhood games began to instruct me beneath the fun. Duck-Duck-Goose and Tag taught me to touch without harming. Jump Rope taught me to jump into the action without getting slapped in the face, and to leap over obstacles. Dodge Ball taught me avoidance maneuvers, to get out of the way of harmful objects. Red Light-Green Light was my first driving lesson, although learned imperfectly and reinforced years later by my first traffic citation. Simon Says was my first taste of having a boss other than my parents. And searching games, such as Hide and Seek and Easter Egg Hunts, sharpened my searching skills and taught me to persevere in the hunt for various objects that I knew were there, although hidden from view, like tomatoes in an enormous tomato patch.

I began to learn about loss early, too. The goldfish that Mom and Dad ceremoniously buried in the backyard, for my benefit, rather than flushing it, as they would have preferred. The parakeet found "sleeping" one day in the bottom of its cage. The numerous, beloved furry pets that drifted into, and then inevitably out of, my life over the years.

As I grew older, I learned that people, too, have a shelf life. I tended to avoid funerals, as many do out of fear or uncertainty, or perhaps denial. I attended my first one, my grandfather's, when I was in my early 20's, and finally learned to fully say goodbye, adding the lesson of loss to the others meant to equip me for life on my own, out of the safe harbor of Mom and Dad and home.

Because the Master Architect uniquely structures life's journey for each participant, I have only my own experience as a reference. Here is what I have learned so far:

- Life is actually not a game at all. It is an interactive journey, not designed to be primarily competitive like games created by the limited minds of men.

- Recognition is earned, not for besting an opponent, but for helping out fellow travelers and adhering to the established guidelines as defined by the Creator.

- Each participant has his own path unlike any other, and a predetermined but undisclosed distance to cover.

- For most of the journey's duration, the destination is hidden from view, although in some cases, particularly when the journey has been difficult or lengthy, it becomes visible ahead in the distance. Sometimes a participant reaches it almost without awareness, suddenly finding himself at his path's end.

- The path layout is complicated, and often changes

without warning. Parts of the path are level and smooth, and the traveling is easy. But then the path will change to a steep, uphill grade, or dip down into dark, difficult places.

- The course is immutable, although from time to time I have attempted to bargain with the Architect for modifications - to lengthen someone's path, to allow me to go back and do over, and once, to leap ahead to my own destination. But He is in control, and will not be swayed. Sometimes, further down the path the reason became clear. More often, it remained a mystery, demanding faith in His wisdom.

- I frequently find myself traveling closely parallel paths alongside others on their journey, as if the roads have converged for a time. Within these alliances, I find companionship, humor, and assistance when I inevitably stumble or must travel a difficult portion of the path. Alliances can last many years, sometimes the majority of the journey's duration, and it is easy to forget that we each must begin and end alone, until a loss reminds us again.

- The further the distance of our individual path, the more we must say farewell, and the more solitary the remainder of our journey. Sometimes I have thought that it would be better to avoid forming friendships and be spared the inevitable goodbyes. But then I remember the enduring aspect that alliances provide to bridge the path boundaries. More permanent than the sadness of goodbye is the comfort found in memories of all those who shared a portion of my journey.

Recently, one of my good friends reached the end of his path unexpectedly on a sunny summer afternoon. Measured by the love and friendship left behind, his journey was a great success.

All of those who traveled near him will miss his company, his strength, and his assistance at difficult points in our own journeys. We will remember the things he taught us, and the beauty he showed us through his love of photography. We will carry his memory gently in our hearts, among the memories of all the dear ones waiting for us when we each reach our own destination.

In my mind's eye, I can picture him at journey's end, pointing out areas for improvement to the Master Architect, who is listening with great interest and taking his suggestions under consideration.

See you at the end of the path, Kurt.

[In memory of my friend, Kurt P. Mezger, 12/19/56 – 8/22/12]

Judi Kotwas

19: HE SHINES

"Let your light shine within you so that it can shine on someone else. Let your light shine." - Oprah Winfrey

Most of my readers know that I have been a fiercely loyal fan of Adam Lambert ever since his musical introduction to the world on American Idol three years ago. I love his music, his personality, and the way he makes a positive difference in the world. He is handsome, charismatic, and limitlessly talented, one of the great musical voices of our time, as many musicians in the industry have acknowledged, although the media inexplicably and persistently passes him over for the likes of Justin Bieber. Go figure.

Adam's fan base, dubbed "Glamberts," encompasses a diverse demographic united by the common thread of our loyalty to, and love of, Adam. It is so easy to strike up a conversation with a fellow Glambert at one of Adam's concerts; in seemingly no time, we are bonding as if longtime friends. Some of his richer fans follow him all over the world to attend his concerts, and I would, too, if I had the money. Instead, I wait for performances close to home, paying outlandish prices to ticket scalpers for seats as close to the stage as possible.

In September, while on a short trip to Las Vegas with my daughter, Jess, I found out that Adam had scheduled a charity concert in Washington, D.C. to support the Maryland Equality in Marriage question that would be on the November ballot. He would fly in on a Tuesday for a single performance at a small venue, then fly home the same night. The tickets went on sale while we were in Vegas, and the concert would be 3 days after our return. I had to wait until I returned home to try for tickets, and expected them to sell out before I could get there.

We returned from Vegas on a Saturday night. The next day, Sunday, I went on-line to check for tickets. The meet-and-greets were, of course, already gone. As badly as I wanted to meet Adam, to date I have had no luck getting meet-and-greet tickets, unwilling to pay the $1000-or-more per ticket that scalpers demanded. So I bought three VIP tickets, and convinced my daughter and my 17-year-old friend, Brian, both also devoted Adam Lambert fans, that the loss of sleep on a weeknight would be a small price to pay for the experience of seeing Adam perform in a smaller, more intimate club setting.

By the time Brian and Jess both got home from work and we fought rush-hour traffic to the club, we had missed the early entry time that the VIP tickets had guaranteed us. We found our way into the club, and although the front couple of rows were already filled in, we found places in the second floor balcony all the way at one end, just over the stage. If I had climbed over the rail and jumped, I would have broken both legs on the actual stage. Good location.

The excitement in the club was palpable, and intensified as the time approached for the show to begin. Then, Adam appeared, taking the stage from our side. I watched as the top of his head passed directly below. He has a great head of hair, by the way. He was devastatingly attractive as always, dressed in a fanciful blend of dressy and casual - suit and t-shirt, dress shoes and no socks – and because Adam loves to change up his look, his usually jet-black hair was dyed what he described as "antique silver."

The performance was one of the best I had seen, with less showiness – no laser lights or glittery makeup or costumes – and more spontaneity and playfulness. Adam was relaxed, interacting with the small audience, ad-libbing and joking. As always, he played the entire stage, returning frequently to our end. I leaned so far over the rail, stretching my hand toward him, that once or twice I was in probable danger of tumbling over and landing in a heap on top of him, but he trustingly reached up toward us, and even blew a kiss or two. It was the concert of my lifetime. When he and the band exited the stage (at our end), I could just see him standing, waiting, as the audience called for an encore. I leaned over the rail, clasping my hands in the traditional "begging" posture, and yelled "Please, Adam... just one more song … pretty please…!" OK, he probably couldn't hear just me, but a fan can fan-tasize... Adam and his band returned to the stage for an enormously satisfying encore performance, and then the show was over.

Brian, who has had great experience and phenomenal luck meeting celebrities, convinced us to wait by the "stage door" to possibly meet Adam after the show. I didn't expect to have such luck, especially since meet-and-greet tickets had been sold and a pre-show meet-and-greet had already been held for the lucky ticket holders. As we waited in the crowd, we heard that club security had planned for him to go directly to the van and to the airport. Still, we waited. Perhaps we could catch a glimpse of him in the van, and perhaps he would wave as they went by. We Glamberts are eager for any crumbs we can glean, believe me.

After about 45 minutes, club security had us all line up against the wall of the building, in single file. At first we thought that perhaps they intended to walk Adam past us to a van parked by the front entrance. And then, we found out that sometimes, if you are patient and willing to wait out in the evening chill and the wind and the humidity, luck smiles down upon you. Adam had convinced security to change the original plan, so that he could meet his fans. Some fans pushed and shoved to be at the front of the line.

We chose the higher path, and went toward the end of the line/ As we watched, security personnel placed a barrier in place in the alleyway leading to the stage door, just in front of the first fan in line, and stationed themselves around it. And then, Adam walked up to the barrier, and my world tilted on its axis for an instant before shifting into the realm of surrealism as we waited to meet him.

Outwardly I remained polite and patient, the perfect fan, while inwardly smothering the wildly-writhing, irrational urge to knock everyone aside and run toward him. I momentarily contented myself with watching as he greeted each fan in front of me in line. Adam looked wonderful, his hair appearing softly touchable and shining in the light, but impervious to the brisk, humid wind that had unrelentingly disheveled everyone in line, flattening my hair against my head into a distinctly unflattering profile as it ruffled others' into wild disarray. He leaned over the barrier to make contact with each fan in some manner – hugging, shaking hands, drawing close for photographs, appearing unrushed, although the line kept moving.

Slowly, we closed the distance to him. Feeling ridiculously like a star-struck teenager, I began to wonder how nervous I would be when meeting him. I hoped for composure and perhaps intelligible vocal ability.

Then the last person in front of me stepped away, and I stood face to face with my musical idol, a man who owns so much of my respect and admiration, along with a small corner of my heart. His smile was warm and genuine, and his eyes telegraphed a welcome. Perhaps he recognized the wacky middle-aged lady in the bright red jacket who had spent most of the concert leaning over the second-level railing perilously close to his head, or maybe he liked my homemade, rhinestone-studded "I Love Adam Lambert" tee. It's more likely that he just loves all of his fans this way.

He leaned down over the security barrier, and my nervousness just fell away. Suddenly I was saying hello to a long-time dear friend. His ability to put people at ease is part of the magic that is Adam. He said "Hi" in his off-stage voice, tenor-pitched and soft. I stepped closer, and without thinking or asking permission, hugged him, and whispered into his ear, "Thank you for this. I know you must be tired." (He had, after all, flown in from California that day for this one-day engagement.) He drew back a bit and paused for a beat, eyebrows raised slightly in surprise, then smiled and said, "Oh! Well, you are more than welcome." I wondered how often anyone considered his feelings over their own.

We exchanged a few words, Brian took a quick photo of us, and then I shook Adam's hand, thanking him again for his music. I had long dreamed of meeting Adam Lambert face to face, and was not disappointed. He is even more charming and personable than I had hoped, a true "nice guy," who gives his entire attention to each person that he meets.

I can comprehend that this story may seem trivial to most. But for me, that small moment in time fulfilled a dream, and created a lasting memory.

He shines.

Judi Kotwas

20: A PAIN WHERE A PILL CAN'T REACH

"If you keep doing what you've always done, you'll keep getting what you've always gotten." - *Buckminster "Bucky" Fuller*

I'm fascinated by words, and the way meanings can change with the times. Growing up, I learned catch phrases that wove themselves into my vocabulary. For example, "hip" was an adjective describing someone with ultimate coolness, savvy and sophistication - the opposite of today's "noob." One of my favorites was the now-outdated phrase, "a pain where a pill can't reach," now superseded by today's more crass "pain in the ass." Both describe a relentless nuisance or source of annoyance or trouble. All of these have recently taken on more literal, personal significance.

"Hip" is now a noun. My left one harbors the pain where a pill can't reach. She is Ms. Hip-Hyde, a bone-on-bone, limited-range-of-motion, arthritis-ravaged angry source of unrelenting, deep-down aches punctuated by frequent lightning bolts of pain. Short of narcotics, no medication can reach deep enough to muffle the misery, let alone snuff it out. And for the past several weeks, no longer content with disrupting daytime activity, Ms. Hip-Hyde has taken on the sinister personality of an unwelcome night prowler, rudely barging into the predawn hours to steal away comfort and sleep nearly every night, and compelling me to function on cat-naps and caffeine.

A recent motor oil ad campaign described someone who never changes the oil in the car as an "engine killer." By parallel logic, I have to describe myself as a "joint killer." A lifetime of too much weight gain, not enough healthy activity, and too much junk food got me into this predicament.

I ignored the warning signals that began a few years back - the persistent, escalating aches whose barks of complaint could be muffled by Tylenol or Aleve, and the occasional "hitch in my get-along" that caused a slight limp for a day or two until "something shifted," effortless walking resumed, and pain was forgotten.

Just before retirement, I developed a new little pang. For many months I ignored it, although a "shift" never occurred, and gradually my limp became more noticeable.

Last spring, nearly a year after retirement, when gardening season arrived I found many of the usual tasks more difficult and painful, but hoped that the "shift" would come along and life would return to normal. I began snatching at pieces of normalcy like a mouse stealing cheese tidbits from the trap while trying to avoid the snap of pain waiting to strike, gradually hobbling more slowly and painfully through each day. Many of the simple summer pleasures of retirement - hours in the garden, wild berry-gathering in the pasture and meadow, long walks in our woods – turned into trials of endurance.

One day, I walked out to my painting cabin, still under construction, and barely made it back, bent over like Quasimodo. I had to face the fact that something had to be done. Life is too short for hours, days, weeks and months to be squandered on a fixable condition.

My family physician ordered x-rays and an orthopedic consultation, but even with the pain of deterioration shouting its presence, I was not prepared to hear that it was time for a hip replacement. Why, I was MUCH too young for that – or maybe not. But surely there was a less radical solution; Hippocrates himself believed that the natural force within us is the first, greatest step to wellness. Perhaps a conservative strategy could postpone surgery… this is the well-traveled path of denial that so many walk, both before and after me; we want to believe that a lifetime of neglect and bad habits can be reversed by turning things around at the eleventh hour.

So I began my own plan. On a healthier diet, I lost a few pounds. More exercise was a bigger hurdle, because I truly hate exercise - in fact, there is a greeting card that perfectly describes how I feel: "Banging your head against the wall burns 150 calories an hour – and I'd still rather do that than work out." But still, I tried to up my activity level, only to learn that there isn't much you can do with one hip that has lost significant flexibility and range of motion, and continues to deteriorate.

Putting a sock on the left foot became nearly impossible, as did painting toenails on that side. OK, this was getting serious. I decided to try a holistic alternative that I've always wanted to try – Chiropractic. Based on the principle that everything in the body is interconnected, chiropractic methods involve the patient as an active participant, aiding the body in healing itself. Through friends' recommendations, I found a caring, competent chiropractor, Dr. W., near home and began chiropractic adjustments three times a week.

The most enjoyable aspect of these sessions was the roller bed that I immediately nicknamed "Old Creaky." Lying on my back on Old Creaky, I contemplated the ceiling tiles as shiatsu-like rollers moved from my neck to the base of my spine, a gentle, giant fist in an undulating pattern, repeated in firm yet comforting waves of rolling pressure at a slow, peaceful pace. The roller mechanisms creaked and groaned like an old ship rocking on the ocean waves, lulling me into a sort of Zen-like meditative state. All of the patients loved Old Creaky. Everyone wished, at the end of the treatment, that they could have just another minute or two. I suggested to the chiropractor that he could generate a little extra income by installing a coin machine, like you see on those kiddy rides outside the grocery store. We would all gladly attend our adjustment sessions with pockets full of quarters.

After several weeks of chiropractic, my neck and back were the best they had been in years, but Ms. Hip-Hyde resisted Dr. W's best efforts, continuing her relentless downward spiral of increasing pain and stiffness. To add to the misery, after carrying more than its share of the load for all the months of limping, my right foot began hurting into the arch, making daily activities even more painful and challenging. I bought arch supports and a cane, pink embellished with rhinestones, but still a cane, and began using it, hating every old-lady moment and nuance of it.

It was time to face the fact that some things, once broken, cannot be fixed with determination and perseverance, and the body's ability to heal itself cannot always triumph over years of neglect. It was time for the "joint killer" to seek further help.

Judi Kotwas

21: PURPLE HAZE

"Purple haze all around, Don't know if I'm coming up or down..." – Jimi Hendrix

2013 is off to a good start for me.

Sometimes it seems that everything is going wrong, but then if you wait a while, the cosmic scales eventually swing the other way and balance everything out. You look around and realize that "God's in His heaven, all's right with the world." (Robert Browning, "Pippa's Song")

That's how it seems now. 2012 ended on a low note, but now I am on the road to recovery from total hip replacement surgery two weeks ago, and last week, although pain medication threw out a foggy screen to blur the edges of memory somewhat, I was still able to enjoy watching my home football team, the Baltimore Ravens, play in Super Bowl XLVII. It's all good.

This seems like an opportune time to buy a lottery ticket.

I ended 2012 with pain and uncertainty. The journey to hip replacement surgery was difficult - convoluted, painful and humbling, with stages of denial and ultimate acceptance that paralleled the Kubler-Ross Five Stages of Grief. I suppose we must mourn, on some level, the loss of any part or piece that must be left behind by the side of the path.   But there were bright spots along the way. I was fortunate to find the right surgeon, the right team, and the right place.

My chiropractor, Dr. W., first told me about Dr. E., an orthopedic surgeon with a solid reputation for successful joint replacements. With that seed planted, each time Dr. E's name came up in conversations with doctors, friends and former patients, his reputation preceded him. There was not one negative comment. My physician described him as THE "hip man," and told me that I would "love him." Her nurse, who worked with him for a period of time, shared anecdotes and enthusiastically assured me that I would "love him."

It was fascinating and reassuring that people thought so highly of him that the comments centered around not just competency or skill, but "love." Any surgeon who merited such high praise from all fronts was someone I wanted to meet. My physician's office scheduled a consultation a week before Christmas, and I began mental preparation for a multi-day hospital stay, painful recovery, long list of restrictions, and several months of rehabilitation.

At the consultation, my husband and I listened as the surgeon and his assistant described the procedure - a newer, less invasive hip replacement technique with shorter hospital stay, much faster recovery than the traditional surgery, and superior results. Good news for a change! Even better, surgery would be performed at the orthopedic practice's own small hospital that boasted such amenities as decent food and flat screen TV's in private rooms. Sort of like a mini spa vacation, with pain and hard work thrown in to keep it interesting. We booked the first opening in the surgical schedule, six weeks ahead.

Six weeks may seem short, but the ever-present, increasing pain and nights of broken, inadequate sleep punctuated the countdown to surgery and caused the days to drag by, even with lab work, pre-surgical screening appointments, and the Christmas holidays providing breaks in the waiting.

I struggled through Christmas shopping, decorating and other preparations, scraping by on catnaps and caffeine, both anticipating and fearing the other "big day" looming ahead. I worried about details beyond my control, and packed my little suitcase for the hospital stay. I hobbled through the waiting days and sleepless nights, counting down the slow-moving hours in a dark parody of a small child awaiting a second Christmas morning.

The last few days were the most difficult, with pre-surgical protocols ruling out pain medications, hot baths, lotions, creams and other small comforts. I discovered that The Pain Where A Pill Can't Reach laughs out loud at a dose of Tylenol, the only medication I was permitted. I walked the halls in the predawn, dark hours like the new resident ghost.

Christmas morning always arrives eventually, and so did the day of surgery. Normally I am in agreement with my favorite musical pop artist, Adam Lambert, who has said, "my makeup is my armor," but medical protocol trumps vanity, modesty, privacy and artifice. On the morning of surgery, I reviewed the surgical protocol checklist: No food or water; no makeup; no hair products or creams or lotions, no nail polish, jewelry, or adornment of any kind. The stripped down version of me, seldom revealed to anyone - very clean, plain-jane and vulnerable with fine, flyaway "dandelion" hair - limped into the hospital lobby and up to the check-in desk with only large sunglasses to hide behind.

Check-in and pre-op preparation were quick and efficient, passing in a blur. I remember being wheeled into the surgical suite and introduced to each member of my surgical team. And then - nothing, until waking in recovery, cocooned in warm blankets and floating on a dizzying cloud of drug-induced fogginess.

By dinnertime, I was tucked into a comfy hospital bed, so glad to see my husband's smiling face. We ordered dinner from the room-service-style menu –

fish, veggies, and chocolate cake for him; chicken broth and Pepsi for me.

The hospital was one of the best, as hospitals go, but there's no place like home, after all. Since the length of hospital stay was based on achievement of physical therapy goals, I focused all my efforts into doing well at the therapy sessions so I could return to my own bed, bathroom and TV. Less than 24 hours after surgery, I was walking the halls on my walker and learning to climb stairs and get in and out of cars. Less than 48 hours after surgery, I was released to go home, feeling like I had "aced" a crucial exam.

Mike took vacation the first week of my recovery and became my personal slave boy, fetching ice bags and medication, dealing with cat care, laundry, cooking, shopping, and a grumpy, groggy wife. By the end of the week, we were still married and still speaking to each other, so we declared it a success.

On Mike's last night home before returning to work, we were in high spirits. Not only was my recovery going smoothly, it was also Super Bowl Sunday and our home team, the Baltimore Ravens, was contending for the title for the first time in twelve years.

Ravens fans are often described as having a "chip on their shoulders," and that may well be true. Strong emotions live in NFL land. Fans don't just cheer for their favorite team or against their rival; they love or hate. Baltimore had won the football franchise in 1996, and ever since, the Ravens had seemed to be the team all the other fans loved to hate, and refused to take seriously. Even after the Ravens won their first Super Bowl in 2001, critics continued the disparaging remarks. So-called experts who persistently underestimated the Ravens' abilities nearly always forecasted them as the underdogs in any contest.

The Ravens' presence in this year's Super Bowl came as a surprise to all but their fans. In every game throughout this year's playoffs, the Ravens had been picked to lose – yet game after game, they had beaten the odds, and against all predictions they were in the final game of the season, playing for the world championship title. From somewhere, they had found a special spark that carried them through when it seemed they had little or no chance of victory. Perhaps their motivation was the imminent retirement of one of their key players – Ray Lewis – at the end of the season. Ray Lewis had been the spirit and motivation for the team since their beginning 17 years ago, and more than anything, he wanted to finish his career on a high note with one more Super Bowl victory for the fans and for his beloved team.

As in every other game of the season, the experts were all betting against the Ravens. We waited for the game to start, hoping to beat the odds one more time, and wondering if the Ravens had one more win in them. I scrounged my wardrobe for Ravens' colors – purple and black – and found something to wear while watching the big game. Mike began making "football food" as we waited for game time. And then the action began. The game was a cliffhanger, one for the record books, with an unprecedented power outage and 34-minute delay mid-game thrown in for added suspense. To my annoyance, although the Ravens led in points from beginning to end, the announcers continued to predict a loss, citing the skill of the opposing team. From time to time, we shouted back at the TV, sometimes muting the volume to stop ourselves from throwing something at the screen out of frustration. Ah, football.

The suspense lasted into the final seconds of the game, when the Ravens came through for Ray and for all of their fans, managing to hold off the opposing team and win the game! Like many of their victories this season, it wasn't pretty, but it was a win – the biggest one of all. A purple blizzard of confetti showered down, blanketing the players and the field. I envisioned countless Ravens fans at countless Super Bowl parties shrieking with joy, and the bet-placers in Las Vegas crying big, wet tears at the money lost on those experts' predictions.

Three days later, on a Tuesday afternoon, I watched the Ravens' victory parade on television. More than 200,000 Ravens fans welcomed the team home, lining the parade route along the streets of downtown Baltimore, pressing in to congratulate the players who rode Humvees from City Hall to their home stadium for the official celebration. Ray Lewis rode in the last vehicle, holding the championship trophy high for all to see. It was the largest fan turnout for any Super Bowl winning team, in any city, ever. The team was overwhelmed by the outpouring of fan love, and Baltimore glowed purple for their world champion Ravens. .

A Ravens world championship, and my hip on the mend.

2013 is off to a good start for me.

22: SANCTUARY

"It is only when we silence the blaring sounds of our daily existence that we can finally hear the whispers of truth that life reveals to us." – K. T. Jong

On a sunlight-saturated, unseasonably cool morning in mid-May, I am writing this while seated at a small, gently aged pine desk in front of a window that frames a view of trees, rocky outcroppings and rolling, grassy land. I am inside my newly completed painting studio, the fulfillment of a small, lifelong dream.

Nearly three years ago, we located the perfect setting across the stream from the house, a small, shady alcove tucked along the side of a grassy egress leading up into the hidden meadow at the leading edge of the woods, secluded and out of view of the road. From the meadow above, the ground sloped down all the way to the stream far below. Rock ledges, undergrowth and small trees formed a picturesque, natural wall at the back of the alcove. The location was less than a quarter mile walk from the house, and far enough removed from the road to fade the harsh sounds of traffic into a barely discernible whisper

We broke ground on a sunny summer afternoon, using the tractor front loader to roughly dig out and level the site, and began to plan the details. The building would have to be small to fit the alcove, which was only about 9 x 12 feet. I wanted more than a simple, rustic cabin in the woods – something low maintenance, with vinyl siding, double-hung vinyl windows, and a "real" door with locks; something insulated against drafts and tight against insect invasions. I hoped for a loft at one end. We began the hunt for scavenged and used materials.

Progress was sometimes slow, often taking a necessary back seat to other tasks and conditions – careers, endless gardening tasks in the warm months, inhospitable weather in the cold months. The remoteness of the location presented additional challenges, such as the logistics of moving countless loads of building materials to and from the site, and running electricity through 500 feet of extension cord from the barn for the power tools needed for the project.

Most of the construction work fell to my husband, with occasional, much-appreciated assistance from family and friends. I helped where I could, but my forte is decorating and painting, not construction and heavy lifting. .

But dreams are worth waiting for, and projects do finally reach completion. After countless hours of work, frustration, triumphs, setbacks, blood and sweat (mostly my husband's) and tears (totally mine), I sit here in my little cabin. It is all that I had hoped for, and more - irresistibly cozy and welcoming, with charming details in every direction. Soft gray vinyl siding covers the exterior, with a roof made from tin roofing left over from the new barn roof several years ago. A small deck runs across the front of the cabin and is just wide enough to accommodate my small butterfly-shaped wrought iron chair and matching flower-shaped table. There are four double-hung windows, and two decorative windows at the roof peaks at each end – one a crescent shape, and the one over the loft a leaded glass octagonal window.

Inside, the décor is undeniably girly (since this was my major contribution to the project): Pale, muted aqua walls and crisp white trim. A shaggy blue-green rug atop a dark blue-green linoleum floor, in front of a old white loveseat draped with a patchwork quilt and piled with pillows. Delicate, white lace curtains welcoming in the sunlight, which streams in on all sides in exuberant abundance. A small, white ceiling fan nestled at the roof peak. In one corner, not yet completed, will be a ceramic-tile hearth on which will sit a lovely little silver-blue Victorian woodstove that we discovered at a local restoration hardware warehouse. .

The focal point is the loft, high enough that my easel fits under it in one corner and I can stand up under it (although my husband can't). It runs the 8-foot width of the cabin at one end, and is about 2-1/2 feet deep, large enough to store frames and canvases, and also large enough to nestle into with a good book on a quiet, rainy afternoon under that lovely tin roof upon which the rain will play a soothing rhythm. The loft walls, and the wall up at the roof peak on the opposite end of the cabin, are dressed in wallpaper featuring bouquets of violets and other spring flowers in soft, pastel watercolor-like shades. Wallpapering over bare plywood was a challenge, but well worth the effort when viewing the results.

On the front wall, just inside the door and under the front window framing a view of blue sky through the tree branches, sits a small, white desk that contains a potpourri of supplies and bits and pieces, as well as faint echoes of my daughter's long-ago childhood. I remember sitting cross-legged on the utility room floor with white enamel and brush, late one evening so many years ago, painting this little desk and carefully attaching the white ceramic drawer knobs with the little pink roses on them. I had nearly forgotten the desk until, while searching for suitable furnishings for the cabin, I rediscovered it in the storage area of our large bank barn, and knew immediately that it was the right combination of size and misty memories of years gone by to warrant inclusion in my new little retreat. Each time it comes into view when I swing open the cabin door, I imagine my sweet little blonde child of yesterday, drawing pictures and reading books while seated at it. Some days I miss that sweet little girl so much, until I glimpse her again in my grown daughter's beautiful blue eyes.

For the past few weeks, I have made daily trips out to the cabin to accomplish and cross off finishing chores on my long list of final details - painting, cleaning, wallpapering and moving in possessions. Some days I packed a lunch and spent most of the day there. In my little UTV, it is a somewhat circuitous but scenic overland drive that skirts the perimeter of our small, young orchard. In good weather and with no excess cargo, it is a pleasant walk, across a small footbridge spanning our stream, then along the opposite bank around a gentle curve where trees and undergrowth provide a natural privacy screen. Each time I round that final bend and the cabin comes into view, I can't help but smile.

So I sit here at the little desk, in my newly completed cabin, writing the old-fashioned way with pen and paper, to be transferred later to my computer. When I pause to gaze out of the window directly in front of me, I can see the top of my flower table out on the deck, and beyond it, through the screen of budding spring greenery, the lower part of our sunlit pasture down the hill and over the stream. A soft breeze ruffles the leaves of a tree just across the grassy access path out front. I feel safe, nurtured by the evidence of my husband's love surrounding me in this haven that he created for me, and at peace.

A few tasks remain to be completed: Power for lamps and the ceiling fan is still via 500 feet of extension cord. We need to find a screen door. The loft ladder is still under construction. The hearth is not installed. The woodstove and pipe must be installed and connected.

But all of that is tolerable for now. I am here at last, making it into my own space a little more each day. The beauty and solitude nourish my soul and fuel my creativity. Words flow more easily to paper here, from thoughts undistracted by everyday chores and intrusive sounds.

Earlier today, I completed the furnishings with my easel, brushes and paint supplies, now neatly organized in a small bookcase. The easel stands expectantly in its allocated location, in the corner under the loft, just to my left as I sit at the little white desk. A fresh, new canvas stands upon it, the palettes, brushes and paints are lined up nearby, and half-formed images, stored away for so long in my mind, queue up for their long-anticipated journey to canvas.

After nearly a decade of exile in boxes and corners of the attic and basement, these old familiar friends whisper that it is time to resume the journey.

23: CAT IS A HALO
(A Tribute to Zack)

"There is no death, only a change of worlds."
- Chief Seattle

A few days ago, Mike and I stroked our little 2-year-old cat, Zack, spoke softly to him, and kissed his furry gray head as he closed his bright green eyes for the last time, the veterinarian's administered injections mercifully ending his time of suffering. Zack was a victim of a disease that is on the unfortunate rise in the world of house cats. FIP (Feline Infectious Peritonitis) strikes down young cats when a common, somewhat innocuous feline virus mutates into its lethal alter-ego and unleashes a cruel disease with no cure or effective treatment and no possibility of survival, leaving the cat's stunned caretakers with no humane choice except euthanasia.

Zack was the youngest of our three cats, and the most personable, greeting strangers and friends alike with unguarded enthusiasm and affection.   He, like the other two cats, Joe and Izzy, was a rescue cat, but while the other two came to us literally out of the woods, having endured hunger, probable dangers and possible abuse, Zack had been rescued by a shelter when his entire litter was only a few days old and near death, so he had no memory of cruelty or unkindness. He was not beautiful by cat show standards, built low to the ground with a big gray body and a round white belly that made his head appear too small for the rest of him. His funny little face was gray with a white stripe running crookedly down his nose, as if the artist who painted it had a shaky hand that day. But his eyes were beautiful - luminous, bright, and the greenest I have ever seen on a cat. His tail was thin, but so cute as it shivered with delight each morning when he greeted us in the bathroom.

All cats have quirks and mannerisms that define their uniqueness, and Zack was no exception. He was our loveable knucklehead, our fearless clown, who regularly broke the house rules and then playfully charmed us out of being angry with him. I remember the time I spotted a gray and white cat in the front yard and thought, "gee, that cat looks like Zack", then realized it WAS Zack. A quick search of the house uncovered his escape route in the basement: an old window with loose glass panes, a cat-bump, and presto, he had made his break. I opened the front door and hollered at him to get inside, and he obeyed; but instead of coming through the nearby front door, he ran around the side of the house and jumped back in through the pane-less window. (I could only shake my head and guess at how many times he had performed this action.) Then he stood watching as I piled boxes in front of the window to keep him contained until Mike could get home from work and replace the glass.

Zack was an indoor cat all his life, but never lost the desire and longing to be outdoors. He was always hanging out near the front door, hoping for an opportune moment to slip out. He and our outdoor cat, Izzy, spent many sessions nose to nose at that door, and if the storm door didn't quite close, Izzy would hiss and reach a jet-black paw in through the crack, and Zack would good-naturedly lie down, roll onto his side, and bat back playfully with his gray and white paw, trying to engage her in a game. Zack had no hate or distrust in him and was blissfully ignorant of such traits in anyone else, feline, human or otherwise.

The great love of Zack's life was my husband, Mike. Zack would climb up on Mike's lap and walk up his chest until his whiskers ticked Mike's face, their noses only a millimeter apart, as if Zack wanted to share the very air that he breathed with Favorite Person. Then he would nuzzle Mike's nose and face, and lick Mike's nose lovingly. Zack often climbed up to my face, too, but without the nuzzle-lick-nuzzle. I always knew that Zack loved me, but there was no doubt who Favorite Person was. Mike could not spend bathroom time without Zack pushing open the door and climbing up into his lap to be petted, or lying at his feet. Zack would let Mike carry him around in undignified poses, such as on his back, slung over Mike's shoulder, with his hind legs vee'd in the air and toes spread wide. Zack could spread his toes out wider than any other cat I've ever known.

Sometimes Mike draped Zack over the top of his head and walked around the house. They called this game "Cat is a Hat."

Zack had his rituals with me, too. His favorite was to be a comforting little furry presence during my bubble baths in our big Jacuzzi tub. He was always there, curled up on my towel on the corner seat of the tub, reaching down from time to time to bat at the bubbles.

Cats are masters at hiding symptoms of illness, probably as a survival tactic in the wild. So we were unaware for a time that Zack was ill. Despite his zeppelin-like body, he had always been a picky eater, turning his nose up at the morning canned food that our other indoor cat, Joe, ate with gusto. Zack grazed throughout the day at the two dry food stations in the house, then came for treats each evening. And because he started out rather heavy, the weight loss went unnoticed for a while.

Then one evening, as I petted him, I could feel bones where I hadn't before. I also noticed that Joe, who had always been affectionate with Zack, was beginning to bully him, and that Zack was hiding rather than defending himself. We took Zack to the vet, and were alarmed to find that he was running a fever and had lost considerable weight. We discussed possibilities with the doctor, and FIP was mentioned, but with no definitive test for it, we mutually agreed to try a week of antibiotics and hope for improvement.

As the week progressed, Zack grew more lethargic, ate almost nothing, and slept most of the time, clearly losing ground. At the end of that week, a phone conversation with the vet made it clear where this road was heading. We scheduled Zack's last vet appointment, and began our final days with him.

He spent each night in our room, curled up at the foot of the bed on his fuzzy brown blanket or in the bathroom on the corner of the tub, on my towel that I left there for him. During the day, he slept in those same two places, or in the closet on a soft pile of Mike's clothes. We decided to give him the one thing that would still bring him a little enjoyment, and took him outdoors frequently, where he would chew the grass, occasionally chase a butterfly or bug, and mostly lie in the sunshine on the front porch, sniffing at all the interesting smells around him.

On his last evening with us, he jumped up on the bed where we were watching a ballgame on TV. He came up to me first, walking up my chest to put his face close to mine, whiskers tickling my cheek, sharing the same air, while I petted him gently. Then he went over to Mike, walked up his chest, and laid down there with his face close to Mike's, sharing the same air. He nuzzled Mike, and licked his nose. Zack was saying his goodbyes. After a few minutes, he jumped down, went back into the bathroom and curled up on my towel on the corner of the tub.

Mike rose early the next morning, and while he dressed for work, Zack kept him company in the bathroom, coming over to sit at his feet at the commode. While Mike was at his office, I stayed with Zack throughout the day. I took Zack outside in the post-dawn hours so he could hear the early morning bird song and chew the dew-covered grass. We went outdoors several times that last day, but Zack was growing weak, and spent the time lying in the sunshine on the porch, then finally hiding under my UTV parked near the porch, a clear sign that the end was approaching.

The vet appointment was that afternoon soon after Mike's return home. When the time came, Mike held Zack in his arms for the short car ride while I drove. He carried Zack in to the vet's office and I brought the little box containing Zack's soft, fuzzy brown blanket. The process was quicker than usual because Zack was so much sicker than we had suspected. I believe that Zack had held on that last day waiting for Mike's return. We wrapped him in his soft blanket and brought him home, tucked his favorite toys into the box with him, and laid him to rest next to our other furry babies' graves near the edge of our garden.

Each one is marked by something special: Hobo has a heart-shaped rock; Kashmir, cat of my heart, rests under a pink rose bush; Kahlua (a.k.a. Fur Ball) has a beautiful white hibiscus plant, as exotic in looks as she was. Zack, our little funny-faced clown, will have a holly bush, in memory of all the holly leaves and plastic red berries that he pulled off the stair banister garland at Christmas and batted around the house.

Zack is now in the arms of his heavenly caretakers, tickling their faces with his whiskers as he shares the same air, and teaching them how to play his favorite games. I predict the most popular one will be "Cat is a Hat," although in Heaven they'll probably call it "Cat is a Halo."

He's saving the tail-shivering, nuzzling and nose-licking until he sees Mike again someday.

Bye, Zackity-Zack. We will miss you.

Zack

Judi Kotwas

24: BIRTHDAY REFLECTIONS

"Because time itself is a spiral, something special happens on your birthday each year. The same energy that God invested in you at birth is present again." - *Rabbi Menachem Mendel Schneerson*

On this crisp, autumn morning in mid-October, I'm in my favorite writing spot, seated at the little white desk in my small, cozy cabin in the woods. Lace curtains on the window filter the sight of the trees, and the meadow beyond, into a hazy, dreamlike mosaic of warm fall colors. The ground all around the cabin already wears a carpet of fallen leaves in layers of brown, russet, gold and crimson that seem to echo the sunlight even on overcast days.

Our little black outdoor cat, Izzy, lies curled in my lap, purring softly and blinking up at me through half-closed, sleepy green eyes, occasionally reaching out a jet-black paw to bat softly at the moving pen in my hand. She seems delighted to have discovered this house-like environment where she is permitted inside to warmth, safety and comfort. My little sanctuary doesn't replace her main hangout, my husband Mike's big, airy workshop on the second level of the corn crib, with her food dish and bed, and where Mike's daily presence assures her of regular human companionship and abundant foot pets and jaw scratching. Nor does it supplant her favorite hideout and playground, the large bank barn where she spends the majority of her solitary time. The cabin merely adds another safe harbor with the familiar smells and sounds of her people-family, and she reciprocates with the warm, comforting presence of her furry self.

It is peaceful here in the cabin. The daily pace seems to slow each time I come out here. I feel free to set aside my to-do list, take a deep breath, and reflect on a variety of topics. Autumn is my favorite of all the seasons, perhaps because it is the briefest, or perhaps because, In just a few days, my birthday will be here. I was born at 10:45 in the morning, a civilized hour to be awake, dressed and fully engaged in the day's activities, which means that each year on my birthday I can pause precisely at that moment, on the very threshold of another year, to ponder the events of the past twelve months and to express my gratitude to God and the fates for the new chapter ahead.

Most of my birthdays have been good days. Most have been filled with happy yet ordinary, expected, comfortable events, their details fading with the passing years. For the first 57 years of my life, I shared my birthday with my father, George Wise. As a small child, with the selfishness of the very young I wished for my own birthday cake, not wanting to share, even with my dad. I remember the year that my mother literally drew a line down the center of the cake so I could have my own half all to myself, with pink roses. In later years, I came to cherish having Dad as my birthday buddy.

As I look back at past birthdays, some memories stand out. My 18th birthday took place two months after I began college near a coal-mining town deep in the mountains of West Virginia, 500 miles from home. Finances and a hectic schedule ruled out a trip home, so I experienced my first birthday away from home and family, and my first not having to share with Dad (and wishing I could) in the new, unfamiliar world of college classes, dormitory life, and newly-made friends. I was fortunate. Those new friends made my birthday special with a pizza topped with pepperoni and candles, and small, inexpensive gifts that eased the homesickness and created happy memories that I cherish nearly 50 years later.

The year that I turned 30, I spent my birthday at home, alone with my dear little golden-haired 5-year-old daughter, who was sick with an ear infection, fever and sick stomach.   Self-pity hovered nearby, until it occurred to me that my father had spent HIS 30th birthday in a hospital lounge, waiting for my arrival a few weeks early, rather than celebrating at a party with his friends. I hugged my little girl closer, sang to her, did what I could to make her feel better, and thanked God for her, and for my own parents. It was a good birthday after all.

My 50th birthday came three days after Mike and I married. After a beautiful wedding and reception surrounded by family and friends, the birthday passed with little fanfare, but it would have been selfish and ungrateful to expect any different scenario. I think the marriage was the bigger milestone that year.

In 2004, I had my first birthday without my lifelong birthday buddy. Dad had passed away in January, and even now, my mind shrinks away from memories of that sad, dark day that, without Dad, just didn't feel like a birthday.

My lovely, grown daughter, Jess, took me to afternoon tea for my 60th birthday. We returned to my house late in the afternoon, and when I opened the front door - surprise! Friends and family had come together for a surprise birthday barbecue. I felt loved that day. Very loved.

In 2011, nature herself gave me a unique, beautiful gift - birthday snow, the kind that is hypnotic to watch as it falls in large, feathery flakes. Mike and I cancelled the elaborate dinner reservations that he had planned, and hunkered down at home while 6 inches of fluffy, sparkling snow piled up outside, transforming the landscape outside our farmhouse windows into a silent, picturesque, living birthday card. We made popcorn, watched movies, played games, and had a quiet, fabulous time that I will remember for years to come.

Last year, a hurricane-force storm hit our area on my birthday, complete with torrential rains and tornado warnings. I was home alone because Mike had wisely elected to stay overnight in his office rather than brave nature's fury for the 87-mile commute home. I was tucked under a quilt with a good book when a horrific crash shook the house and jolted me up out of my cozy spot. Had a car hit the house? That's what it sounded like.

I began looking for the source, and soon found it. High winds had brought down a large chunk of the ancient cedar tree in front of our house, demolishing part of the front porch as the huge branches crashed down, and blocking the front door with logs and debris. I took my book, quilt, the cats and some emergency food down to the basement to wait out the rest of the storm. (Happy birthday, dear Juuu-diiii... happy birthday to youuuuuu...). Then our nearest neighbor called to make sure I was okay. He and his wife had seen the tree break and crash down, and knew Mike wasn't home. And just like that, a simple reminder that I wasn't alone on my birthday brought me back to gratitude.

I will be 67 on October 29, 2013. At 10:45 in the morning, I will be sitting in a hospital waiting room, waiting for my dear friend Kathy, who needed someone to drive her, to come out of outpatient surgery. I will pause precisely at that moment, on the very threshold of another year, to ponder the events of the past twelve months and to express my gratitude to God and the fates for the new chapter ahead.

Then I'll take Kathy home, tuck her into her bed, make sure she has pain medication and hot tea or a cold drink and whatever else she needs. I'll do everything I can to make her feel better. And as I drive home, I will thank God for the past year, for the years ahead, for friends who love me and need me, for a family that I cherish, and for a father who now lives in heaven, but who will never be far from my thoughts on our shared birthday.

Happy birthday, Dad.

25: A VICTORIAN TEA

*"Tea is quiet, and our thirst for tea is never far from
our craving for beauty." - James Norwood Pratt*

I used to regard retirement as akin to an unending
vacation with long days of leisure and no
responsibility. That was before I got here. It may be
true for some, but for me, life continues to fill the
hours with an abundance of activity and tasks. One
of my favorite escapes from the hustle and bustle of
daily schedules and to-do lists has become the ritual
of afternoon tea.

I'm a very lucky woman. I had only one child, my
daughter, Jessica. Now that she is grown with
children of her own (my two beautiful little
granddaughters!), she is also my dearest friend, and
we love having the all-too-infrequent afternoons
together, just the two of us, to catch up and reconnect.
She shares my love of afternoon tea, so we partake
whenever we can squeeze it into our two schedules -
sadly, not often enough for either of us.

The first time Jess and I went to a tearoom, I felt
enveloped in the tranquility and leisurely pace. How
indulgent to stretch the customary "lunch hour" (or,
as was more common for me in the work world, the
"lunch half-hour" and sometimes the "no-lunch half-
hour") into two or even three luxurious, unrushed

hours! Jess and I left that first tea feeling both relaxed and energized, ready to resume our busy schedules with smiles on our faces.

Since then, we have been always on the lookout for new tearooms offering high tea, and each time we discover find one, it is like opening a lovely, unexpected gift. By luck, perseverance, and the help of cyber technology, Jess recently discovered a new location in a small, nearby town tucked away in the gentle hills and valleys of south central Pennsylvania.

This year, with Thanksgiving falling on the latest possible date, November 28th, there was less time to prepare for Christmas, yet the same tasks and events to crowd into fewer days. Jess booked our tea for the day after Thanksgiving as a late-birthday celebration for my birthday on October 29th, and fortuitously, it also served to remove us as far as possible from the Black Friday shopping frenzy and the accompanying stress and anxiety. After all, nothing kills a warm pre-Christmas mood quicker than witnessing crazed shoppers trampling each other to possess the last $99 big-screen TV on the shelves. And what better refuge than a leisurely afternoon tea?

And so it was, that we found ourselves, on the day after Thanksgiving, en route to The Victorian Parlor for afternoon tea. I had never been to Spring Grove before, and had to trust my faithful GPS to guide me to it along winding, two-lane rural roads. But once we arrived, we both knew as soon as we walked through the little wrought-iron gate and into The Victorian Parlor that we had stumbled onto a real treasure, brought to life in the oldest building in Spring Grove, painstakingly renovated, furnished and decorated by people who clearly love what they do and are very good at it, with attention to every detail.

We were fortunate to see the tearoom at its most opulent, decorated lavishly and beautifully for Christmas. In any direction that we looked, there were antique Victorian treasures, beautiful furnishings, Christmas trees and garlands, and exquisite, sparkling accents. No space was left untouched and undecorated, yet that threshold between abundant beauty and excess was never crossed. I found myself wishing that I could see what they had done with the rest of the house.

When we came in, we were welcomed warmly by one of the owners, and seated at a table by a wall covered with lovely ladies' hats. Part of the tradition of tea is the wearing of a beautiful, gauzy or feathery hat. In fact, where else can one wear a beautiful hat in this 21st century jeans-clad society? The hats were available to guests who wished to wear them, so of course we each happily began the search for just the right one. I first selected a big, elegant black satin hat, but then decided to leave "sedate" behind and go for "frivolous," settling on a magenta, feather-bedecked beauty. Jess found a chic little ruby-red pillbox-style with delicately drifting black feathers and netting - perfect with her ruby-red sweater and black pants. We were decked out and ready to begin the ritual.

The owners served the guests themselves, and we fell easily into pleasant conversation each time one of them visited our table. We saw pictures of the original building and heard the story of how the tea room came into existence, and Jess and I found ourselves chatting with them about little details of our own lives, such that by the end of the day we felt as if we had made new friends.

Then there was the food. We had anticipated excellent food, and had eaten very little in preparation for it. We were so glad that we were able to eat nearly every bite of our meal. Diets could wait until tomorrow, and dinner this day could be nothing. This meal was worth it. For a surprisingly modest charge, we were served our choice of unlimited, expertly prepared teas from the daily offerings, and a 6-course meal that combined traditional tea items such as scones and finger sandwiches with delectable, contemporary dishes, finishing with a full-sized seasonal dessert.

With full tummies, unfrazzled nerves, and smiles on our faces, our next stop was the gift shop, stocked with so many treasures in a small space that we needed to circle the room three or four times to take it all in. Jess and I have a tradition of buying a new tea cup or teapot each time we visit a new tearoom, and The Victorian Parlor had so much to offer that we struggled to make a choice.

Finally we each found just the right item. Jess chose a lovely, rose-patterned teacup in a classic Victorian silhouette, and I was delighted to find a small teapot in a pattern that matched a favorite cup already in my collection and for which I had searched unsuccessfully until now. These beautiful bone china pieces would bring us back to this day each time we saw them on display in our collections, or used them in our solitary afternoon tea breaks.

We signed the guestbook, exchanged hugs with the owners, who by this time really did seem like newly-found friends, and drove off, resolved to return to The Victorian Parlor soon, and often.

On this journey of life, we all have good days and bad. And every so often, if we are patient and if we are lucky, we get a perfect day. This was a perfect day.

26: NOBODY HERE BUT US CHICKENS

"I may not know much, but I know chicken poop from chicken salad." *- Lyndon B. Johnson*

As I write this, it is New Year's Eve in 2013. We are nearing the end of our 12th year here on the farm. Our little 23 acres has its share of animal, vegetable and mineral inhabitants, but up until now, the animals have consisted of my husband Mike and me, our small collection of pet cats, and the ever-changing wildlife population, of species both known and unknown to us. The gardens, grounds, streams and woods are alive with a generous cornucopia of life forms, from familiar and exotic insects to birds to furry creatures. It seems each year we have seen at least one new bug or critter that we had never seen before.

And now, to kick off the new year, we are preparing to welcome some new residents. Chickens. Did I ever dream of, or anticipate, being a chicken farmer/owner, the stereotypical farm wife in the apron who goes out to "ye olde" henhouse to gather "them-thar" eggs each day and scatters handfuls of cracked corn to the clucking masses around her feet? No. Not really. But now that renovation of the old chicken house is underway in preparation for the imminent arrival of our first five hens, I'm adjusting to the role. Without the comfortably padded figure in

159

the white apron and hair in a bun, though. I'll stick to jeans.

We are inheriting these first five from my son-in-law, Sean, who raised them from babies in an urban setting. These hens are no strangers to me; I have cared for them during vacations, so I already know them, sort of. They know me as the lady who brought them treats of garden corn with delectable worms and bugs (yuck to me and you, but yum to them), so I don't anticipate any get-acquainted difficulties, such as grumpy hens trying to peck the hand that feeds them and tries to collect eggs.

My husband has been busily renovating the old henhouse located between the house and the large bank barn. It was much larger than needed for our new little brood. From its size and the number of nesting boxes and feeding troughs, we figure it probably housed at least several dozen chickens, maybe more, in days gone by. So Mike split the long, rectangular structure into two roughly-square spaces, using old glass doors as the dividing wall and thereby creating a quirky, fascinating interior. In the half closer to the big barns, he took down the roof and walls, leaving the beam structure, and covered it all with heavy-gauge plastic, creating a roomy and much-needed greenhouse that will allow us to get our annual vegetable garden started earlier and also to experiment with some new types of produce. The chickens will probably enjoy looking through the doors from their side into the greenhouse side and wishing they could get in there to gobble the delectable young seedlings and plants just beyond.

On the chicken side, in addition to wiring it for lights and heat, Mike installed a chicken water fountain and created a roomy fenced-in outside pen for our new tenants, with a clever hinged door to provide access from inside the henhouse and to keep them inside when we want them there. He did such a good job that I got him a new Christmas ornament for this year's tree - a greenhouse. I couldn't find one that was half greenhouse and half henhouse. I wonder why?

There is work left to do on the new greenhouse side, but the renovations on the chicken-house side are nearly finished, and the interior, even though half its original size, will still be much larger than the pen being vacated. These hens will probably think it is a poultry palace; in fact, I think we should name it "Poultry Palace," in keeping with our penchant for naming streams, rocks, trees, paths and structures on our little farm. I'll run it by boss-man and see what he thinks.

We don't know a lot about chickens; neither Mike nor I have ever raised them. Through research, I discovered that there are an astonishing number of chicken breeds. Some are named after states - Delaware, New Hampshire, Rhode Island. Some have curly feathers (Frizzles) or soft, downy feathers (Silky chickens). There are Americanas, Andalusians, Cochins, Leghorns (like Foghorn Leghorn in the cartoons?). There are even Polish chickens (OK, no jokes; my husband is Polish). There are breeds I can't even pronounce.

All I know about the ones we are inheriting is that they are brown (maybe New Hampshire Reds?), and that they lay brown eggs - sometimes enormous ones with double yolks, and I'm sure the hens are glad those don't come along every day.

It seems we are right in with the current trend; people are raising chickens in backyards everywhere, in growing numbers. So, fortunately for us chicken-keeping "noobies," reference material was easy to find. So now, we are armed with a book on how to raise chickens, their new digs are almost ready for occupancy, and the feed store is just 2 miles down the road.

I guess I'll go practice my chicken-calling skills so I'm ready when chicken-moving day gets here. But I'm not wearing that apron and bun, and I draw the line at chopping off a chicken's head when she stops laying eggs. I'm no chicken-killer. I only eat the ones in Styrofoam trays from the store.

Somehow, I think these chickens will sense that.

"Here, chick-chick-chick-chick!!"

Judi Kotwas

ABOUT THE AUTHOR

Judi Kotwas retired from the corporate world in April 2011. She and her husband, Mike, live in South Central Pennsylvania on a small farm that they share with their two cats, Izzy, and Joe, a wide variety of wildlife, and coming soon, a small flock of chickens.

Judi is also an amateur landscape artist.

45936495R00108

Made in the USA
San Bernardino, CA
22 February 2017